Dog Days in the Life of the
Miles-Mannered Man

A collection of tall tales, wagging tails,
and tantalizing treats

OTHER TITLES
From Cathy Burnham Martin

The Communication Coach: Business Communication Tips from the Pros (includes Cathy Burnham's *Taming the Media Monster*)

Fifty Years of Fabulous Family Favorites

A Healthier You: Fabulous Ideas to Help You Live a Healthier Life (includes Cathy Burnham Martin's *Healthy Thinking Habits: Seven Attitude Skills Simplified*)

Champagne: *Facts, Fizz, Food & Fun*

Sage, Thyme & Other Life Seasonings: *Perspectives*

Christmas Cookie Classics

Cranberry Cooking

Lobacious Lobster

Dockside Dining: *Round One*

Dockside Dining: *A Second Helping*

Boat Drinks

Dog Days in the Life of the
Miles-Mannered Man
A collection of tall tales, wagging tails, and tantalizing treats

Per the paws of
Miles Martin

Assisted by his human,
Cathy Burnham Martin

Quiet Thunder Publishing
Manchester, NH

www.QTPublishing.com

This title and more are featured in articles at
www.GoodLiving123.com.

Dog Days in the Life of the
Miles-Mannered Man

A collection of tall tales, wagging tails, and tantalizing treats

Copyright © 2013 Quiet Thunder Publishing
Manchester, NH

All rights reserved worldwide. No part of this book may be reproduced in any form or by any means without prior written permission from the publisher or authors, except for the inclusion of brief quotations embodied in critical essays, articles, or reviews. These articles and/or reviews must state the correct title and authors by name.

2006 Family edition: ISBN 978-0-9770711-1-1
2013 eBook edition: ISBN 978-0-9770711-0-4
2013 Paperback edition: ISBN 978-0-9770711-3-5

Published and printed in the United States of America.

Library of Congress Control Number: 2013917476

DEDICATION 🐾

I dedicate this book of memoirs, tidbits and tips to my favorite and first human, Miss Nina. She rescued me as a pup from the doggie orphanage called "Shelter."

She was barely twelve years old, just a puppy herself in human years! I'm glad she had a heart of gold, even then. (And she's as pretty as a speckled pup.) Thanks Ninja!

This is my Nina

Nina and me

Oh, and thanks also to my other humans, Big Dog and Cathy. They take care of me when Nina is away at school. They also take me to visit my Nina and on lots of adventures.

Through this book, they have made me one very special Forever Dog!

I also thank my Grand Poppy and Grammy Burnham... they take care of me whenever Big Dog and Cathy travel to places that just don't interest me much. (They also rescue me from thunder storms and wind storms.) I really do have a great pack! Number One!

I also salute dog and animal lovers everywhere. We know that you have loved critters before us and will love critters after us. But while we are here with you, we are proud to be on duty for you. We four-legged friends do our best to help our humans feel loved, and we feel blessed that you love us!

It's a dog's life – it's awesome!

ABOUT THE AUTHOR

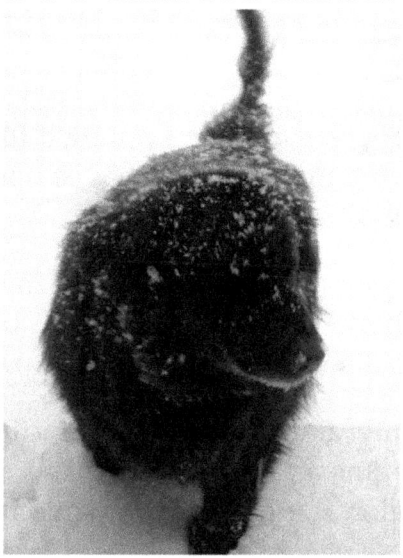

Miles Martin received no formal writing training. Rescued at a young age, he became a proud graduate of the School of Hard Knocks and then was Martinized, where he received brief one-on-one instruction in behavioral management. Miles commented that he continued to remember those lessons well into adulthood.

Always displaying a strong interest in the world around him, Miles has been noted by many as a tireless listener. His also is on record as particularly focusing his keen observation skills on nutrition, nature, and his very closest friends and family.

Miles has been repeatedly mentioned in lists of "the best" and quickly became one of the most actively sought companions ever. His popularity is only outshined by his loyalty and devotion. His expressive personality, eagerness to please, and unquestioned sincerity made the release of this book important to everyone who has ever known and loved Miles Martin.

ACKNOWLEDGEMENTS

Special thanks to:

- Big Dog (The Ronald) for keeping a roof over my head and for loving me when I'm maybe not as neat and tidy as he would like me to be.

- My Cathy human for jotting down my stories. I mean, I would have done it all myself, but I don't have thumbs, so it's very hard to hold the pen.

- My Grammy and Grand Poppy Burnham for visiting me all the time and giving me treats, especially when I am home alone (and getting into mischief).

- Also my Grammy and Grand Poppy Burnham and Aunt June get special thanks for proofreading my chapters for me. (I think I was snoozing during spelling class.)

- My mailman and other delivery folks for all the cookies. You're the best!

- My groomers and friends at the Sendaishi Pet Resort for keeping me gorgeous. It's not easy being a sex symbol, you know!

- My doctors and nurses at the Bedford Animal Hospital and all the assistants who take such good care of me.

- All my great friends who think of me often and call me their Buddy, too! You can never have too many friends, and I am truly grateful.

INTRODUCTION

When I first started writing, I was merely collecting a few stories to share with my Nina in letters while she was away at school. I just kept on keepin' on!

It was hard to select which stories you'd most enjoy reading. Regardless, I know I should humble myself and just go ahead and share, even though some show me off as being rather silly. Also sweet. But they are all true... cross my heart. Sharing them with you makes me as happy as a flea in a doghouse!

I also wanted to include some special features. You know, a few of my favorite recipes, special remembrances, and a look at some other rather high profile pooches. They're not all published writers, like I am now, but just wait till you see the list! They've got some great claims to fame.

So Buckaroos, just sit down on your favorite chair with a big fresh water bowl and a Milk-Bone biscuit and enjoy.

I'm not allowed on the chairs, but this chaise needed a try.

TABLE OF CONTENTS

Page

Dedication		5
About the Author		7
Acknowledgements		8
Introduction		9
Chapter 1	Humans	12
Chapter 2	My Pack	15
Chapter 3	My Favorite Maddie	17
Chapter 4	Brown	19
Chapter 5	The Fed Ex Training Program	21
Chapter 6	Thunder & Lightning	23
Chapter 7	Welcome Home	25
Chapter 8	Dig This!	28
Chapter 9	My Own Apartment	30
Chapter 10	Four-Legged Friends	32
Chapter 11	My Turf	44
Chapter 12	Squirrel Patrol	47
Chapter 13	Duck Flushing	50
Chapter 14	Bird Dog	53
Chapter 15	Fish Stories	58
Chapter 16	On the Record	61
Chapter 17	Toys & Treats	65
Chapter 18	Dog of the Year	68
Chapter 19	Prickly Kitties	71
Chapter 20	Stealth Mode	74
Chapter 21	Good Gardening	77
Chapter 22	Leaf Chasing	79
Chapter 23	Doggie Resort	81
Chapter 24	Signals That I Like You	83

Chapter 25	Circus Dog	85
Chapter 26	Nervous as a Cat	89
Chapter 27	Did You Say "Ride?"	91
Chapter 28	Boating Bowzer	94
Chapter 29	Yoga… My Way	100
Chapter 30	Bone Appetite	102
Chapter 31	Chew Toys	104
Chapter 32	Snow Patrol	107
Chapter 33	Lending a Paw	112
Chapter 34	Major Projects	117
Chapter 35	Working Dog	120
Chapter 36	The Musical Me	124
Chapter 37	Winter Olympics	126
Chapter 38	The Great Carjacking Caper	128
Chapter 39	Attitude Adjustment	131
Chapter 40	The Future	134
Chapter 41	Paws to Remember	138

Extra Treats (because you've been good)

1 – Presidential Pooches	142
2 – Other Famous and Heroic Dogs	149
3 – Miles' Favorite Recipes	163
4 – Dog Jokes with the Miles Paw of Approval	175

Credits and References	198

1
HUMANS

*We give dogs time we can spare,
space we can spare and love we can spare.
And in return, dogs give us their all.
It's the best deal man has ever made.*
--Margery Facklam, American Author

There are humans. And then there are _my_ humans. I like humans, but I reeeally like _my_ humans. They are particularly the ones I live with, but my humans also include all the friends I adopt. You know the type... those super nice people who seem to know instinctively that they should scratch behind my ears and rub my belly.

I've even gotten to like the mailman and the Fed Ex man. Of course, that's probably because I trained them to bring me cookies... or else! (Hee hee!) Now they're my good buddies.

I've also got lots of extended family... like Miss Nina's sister and brothers and my Cathy human's Mom and Dad. I own them, too. Christopher (Big Dog's #1 eldest son), Keira (#1 eldest daughter), and Adam (#1 youngest son) all like to visit me. They give me lots of attention. I like that!

Keira, Dad (Big Dog), Nina, Chris, Adam & Cathy hamming, as usual

And talk about friends! Bow-wow! I must be the richest dog in the land. All my human friends greet me with a big, "Hi Miles!" as soon as they see me. They even ask about me when they haven't seen me for a while.

None of them seem to care one bit that I'm "a rescued" dog and not a pure-bred, show dog Newfoundland. They treat me like a super star!

*Just opening one of my Christmas presents.
(I must be a very good dog... I made Santa's list!)*

These folks are the best... you know the type... like Tony and CJ, Norm, Linda, John, Jackie, Ben, Sandy, Jim, Alden and Lynda, Deb, Steve and Heidi, Jeanne, Patty, Lynn, Ryan, Allen and Nancy, Bill, Bob (who calls me "Miles from Nowhere"), Katie (who was scared of me... at first), Aron and Kim, and Turner, too.

The list goes on and on and on. They are my Buddies with capital B's. I'm one lucky dog. Love me; love my humans.

2
MY PACK

Hi! My name is "No No Bad Dog." What's yours?

These are the folks who live in my house with me. My pack. My #1 human is named Miss Nina. She brought me home when I was a puppy. We have a lot of fun. We're always horsing around. She even likes to wrestle! Sometimes I even let her win.

Then there's Big Dog. He's called a lot of different things, so I don't think he's finalized a real name yet. I've mostly heard him called Ron, but also Ronald, The Ronald, Sir Ronald, Dad, Honey, and Sugar. (I guess that's sort of the same as with me. They call me Miles, but also Pookey, Fang, Good Dog, Best Dog, Dog Face, Milesy, Tippy Toes, Teddy Bear, Smiles, Bowzer, Fuzz-Buster, Fuzzy Face, Babba Louie, Miles-a-matic, and Woofy.

Oh, you know that whole lingo bit, where young people talk opposite what they mean? You know, where "Bad" means good. And words like "Sick" mean super. My Nina even sometimes calls me Ugly, but that's because I'm so cute. So I say, "Thank you!" She likes that.

Answering to so many names, some people ask if I have a split personality. They must not know me. If they knew me, they'd know that I don't have a *split* personality. I have a **GREAT** personality!

Anyway, Ron is the Big Dog. What he says, goes. When Big Dog tries to play, I figure I better let him win out of respect. That means I throw him a few bones now and then, because I could win if I really *wanted* to win.

Then there's my other pack mate. They call her Cathy. She's one cool cat. She feeds me, lets me in and out, lets me in and out, lets me in and out, plays, grooms me, and even towels me off when it's been snowing or raining cats and dogs. We talk a lot too. We don't quite speak the same language, but she seems to follow the conversations. (I'm still teaching her.)

On the other hand, I have learned lots of human words. In addition to all my humans' many expressions of love toward me, I know words like: Ride, Come, Sit, Stay, Ride, Okay, No, Down, Squirrel, Ride, Paw, Lie Down, Fetch, Ride, Out, Yard, and Get Him! "Ride" is, by far, my favorite word. (Oh, you knew that!)

3
MY FAVORITE MADDIE

A dog has one aim in life. To bestow his heart.
                    --J.R. Ackerley, British Author (1914-1986)

If you knew Maddie like I know Maddie, oh, oh, oh what a gal. She's the bee's knees. She works at a place called Spatts, which is one of my humans' favorite restaurants. They go there with my buddies Tony and CJ and Ben and Sandy for these really monster cuts of prime rib, that all the humans say are the best they've had anywhere. (I agree, because they bring me the bones. Hah!)

CJ & Big Dog being served by Maddie

That brings me back to Maddie. She **always** asks about me. She sends my humans home with a doggie bag to beat all doggie bags, too. I mean it's HUGE... filled with bones that the chef just cut prime rib meat off for customers that only wanted a small portion. Yeeee-hahhh! My gain, because there's always LOTS of fabulous prime still on that bone! Just thinking about them makes me as hungry as a bear.

I love those things. In fact, I made Maddie a special "thank you" card once, so she could see that I enjoy my gifts from her. I just hold onto those prime rib bones like big ol' lollypops and pig out.

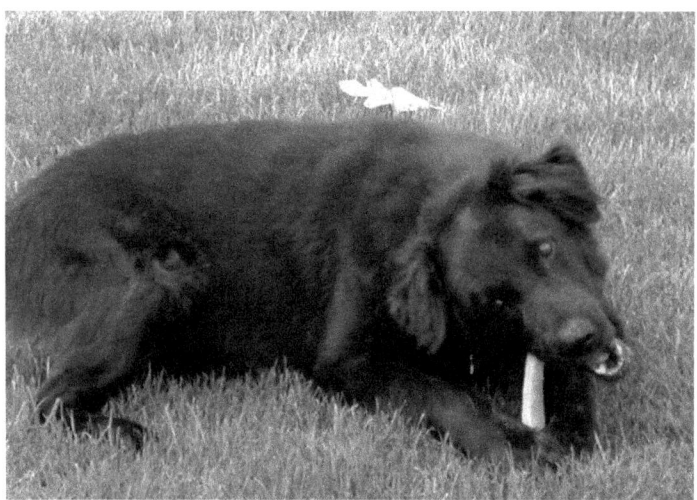
Me, gnawing on what's left of a Spatt's prime rib bone

If you're ever in Manchester, New Hampshire, you've just got to get to Spatts. (Hmmm... I heard my humans say it was sold and is now called Bonsai, but they still have Spatts' amazing prime ribs!) Anyway, it's a family restaurant with fabulous prime... and much more. Yum. Ask for Maddie.

Oh! My Cathy human says you also have to try the stuffed strawberries for dessert. And be sure to take something meaty home for <u>your</u> four-legged love.

4
BROWN

I love a dog. He does nothing for political reasons.
  --Will Rogers, American Humorist (1879-1935)

One of the great mysteries to my humans is why I hate "Brown." Not the color, mind you. It's the UPS truck itself. Ever since I can remember, I can hear a UPS truck a mile away! I try to keep it off the property and out of the neighborhood. It just makes me madder than hornets.

When I hear it at somebody else's house, I bark as loudly as I can so it will know not to come any closer. There are just too many trees. I don't think Brown can hear me sometimes.

That's okay, because just as soon as he's rolling again, I zoom to the street to be sure he won't enter my yard. No, sir! But he's pretty fast, that Brown. He usually zips past my driveway just as I get to the road. Yeaaaaah! He better run away fast!

Now and then I actually win this race. Hah! Brown has to stop! Then he pulls slowly into the driveway and cautiously approaches the house.

I make him pay a price for coming to my house. Yup. (Sometimes you have to take the bull by the horns.) So, I make him choose a package or two from his truck to leave for my humans! Hah! That will teach him! I am the top dog. I am invincible!

So, what can Brown do for me? Just give me a cookie, and I'll let him go on his way. Still, I bark loudly all the while, until he's out of sight.

Man, it's just Brown. If you really want to get my dander up, just try driving into my yard in a UPS truck.

5
THE FED EX TRAINING PROGRAM

Outside of a dog, a book is probably man's best friend.
Inside of a dog, it's too dark to read.
--Julius "Groucho" Marx, American Comedian (1890 – 1977)

Make no bones about it; my ferocious act must be a good one, because I've really intimidated some savvy people, like my Fed Ex Driver. He probably mistook me for a grizzly bear.

He was not impressed, but he was barking up the wrong tree. He should have known right away that I'm really just a big ol' teddy bear. It took a long time for him to figure it out. Till then, he was so nervous sometimes that he didn't dare get out of his truck.

I remember once when he left my humans a notice that he'd tried to make a delivery. He wrote a special note to them: "DOG IN YARD!!!" Yeah, it was all written in big capital letters and three exclamation points! He was nervous. My humans wrote a note back to him: "Leave package with dog!"

So, he did. He still wouldn't get out of his truck though. He just put the box in a giant plastic bag and slowly lowered it out his window to me in the driveway. Then he left, licking his wounded pride.

We went through this a few times until I trained him to give me a cookie. Now he gets out of his truck and everything. (I still haven't been able to train him to stay and play for a while, but I'll keep working on it, doggone it.)

Oh, I heard a funny story about my Fed Ex driver, too. My Big Dog human had gone to Fed Ex to pick up a big box one time, and everybody there knew him because of ME!

They pointed at him and cheered, chanting, "Dog in yard! Dog in yard!" I guess that note and my humans' response had been quite a hit at the Fed Ex office. The tag was still hanging on a bulletin board there. They even said they'd wanted to make a TV commercial using it.

Hmmmm... I wonder who will play me? Probably Brad Pitt or Tom Hanks. Maybe Johnny Depp. Yeahhhh, I'd really like that! This is cool.

Me... my "movie star" close up photo!

6
THUNDER AND LIGHTNING

Inside every Newfoundland, Boxer, Elkhound, and Great Dane is a puppy longing to climb on to your lap.
  --Helen Thomson, California Assemblywoman (1943 -)

My Cathy human doesn't like thunderstorms. Me neither. When they start to get closer and closer I try to stay very close to her... so <u>she</u> won't be as scared, of course. I think she really likes to have me beside her, so I try to virtually attach myself to her side when the thunder booms. (Then she calls me the Velcro Dog!)

At night I even stand guard over her during storms. I position myself between her bedside and the window. Then I face the window so the thunder can't get her. Well, at least I start out facing the window. All the while I'm thinking, "I'll save you!" Kinda like Dudley Do-Right, don't you think!??!

Then the storm gets a little too close... geeeez, it even hurts my eyes with all that lightning flashing. That's when I turn to face her so she can pat my head more easily. I'll admit that I'm a bit less sure that I can save her, but I don't tell her that. That flashing lightning is really quite annoying.

Suddenly, the storm is truly upon us. The crashing is so loud, I think the house will collapse. I just can't stand it anymore. I zoooooom just as fast as I can to the other side of the bed to Big Dog. SAVE ME!!!!!!! (And he does.) Phewwwww.

Finally, the thunder goes away, and we can all go back to sleep. Man, don't ever take me to a bowling alley. If it sounds like thunder, I don't want any part of it.

Okay, okay… I admit it. I can be a real scaredy-cat sometimes… and it's usually just at the moment I wish I could be as strong as a lion.

My humans say that when it comes to thunder, I am truly the Cowardly Lion of Dogs, whatever <u>that</u> means. I just know I'd be fine, if I only had some c-c-c-courage!

7
WELCOME HOME

The average dog has only one request to all human kind: love me.

--Helen Exley,
Author, Editor, Publisher (1943-)

Don't believe for a New York minute any of that malarkey about dogs not having any sense of time. We know perfectly well when you've been gone all day versus gone for five minutes.

Sometimes we manage to pass the time more quickly by playing or getting into a little mischief. Or else we catnap, er, uh, I mean, we dognap... several times, if need be.

Just me waiting... again.

When our humans return, we are just as thrilled if you've been gone a little bit of time as we are if you've been gone for hours. Just know one thing: It's <u>always</u> too long when you're away!

When my humans return, they are always impressed that I come running gleefully to greet them all bright-eyed and bushy-tailed. Count on it. I can recognize the sound of their vehicles long before they approach our yard. I love it when they come home. I am very sad when they drive away... without me, that is. My Cathy human tries to console me when she has to leave me at home by giving me a cookie just before she leaves. I like that a lot. They say that the early bird catches the worm. Well, the birds can have those worms – I tried one once – YUK! I'd much rather have a cookie.

Plus my Cathy human always tells me that they'll be back and reminds me that I'm in charge. Still, I sit there waiting on the porch, and I miss my humans... something fierce. But I know they trust me to protect the place, so I go about my duties.

No matter what, there is nothing greater than hearing them returning home... I gallop straight out to them every time. When they open the car doors I make sure I'm right there to nuzzle them fast and give them doggie kisses and let them pat me. I run around the car, several times if need be, to make sure I properly greet all my humans that are arriving home.

Then I notice that the humans are walking into the house. Hah! Me first! Me first! I'm first in! I zoom past them and get my snout right up to the door.

Oh, yeah... when that door opens, I always like to enter first. This is strictly for protective purposes, of course! I want to make sure that everything is AOK inside.

Well, maybe I want to be sure that I can get to my indoor water bowl before anyone else. (Not that they've ever tried that, but a dog can't be too careful.) I think it's mostly my way of letting them know that I truly do want to go inside with them... right then, not later.

Homecomings are one of the best parts of every day. I miss my humans so very much when they are away. They miss me, too. I know because they almost always greet me with lots of hugs. I say "almost always," because it seems that whenever it's been raining or snowing, they like to smother me with great big towels before hugging me. That's okay, too. I like being patted like crazy... even if it's with towels. Hot diggity dog!

I wish my humans would never ever drive away and leave me... even for just a few minutes. Sigh. But if they must drive away without me, I sure am glad that they always come back. I love welcoming them home again!

Perhaps that's my lesson learned here... I love their homecomings, but I wouldn't _**get**_ to welcome them home if they never left. Sigh.

8
DIG THIS!

Scratch a dog, and you'll find a permanent job.
--Franklin P. Jones, American Businessman (1887-1929)

When you're just plain good at something, you might as well admit it. For me, that special something is digging. They tell me it's because I've got these big, webbed Newfy feet. I prefer to think that I'm just very focused... and strong!

For example, a chipmunk disappears down this little hole in the ground. Well, get ready Chippy, because I'm comin' in. So I start digging – with passion!

That's a Miles Rule. If you're going to do anything, I believe you should really put your whole self into it! I mean if you can't run with the big dogs, stay on the porch, right?

So, I'm gonna get a little dirt on my face. Big deal. In just minutes, there's a brand new, rather spectacular hole in which you could park a small car. (Oh, usually the chipmunk is gone by the time I get there. Man, that is strange, because I can dig really fast. I think these chippies must have back doors to their little hideouts.)

As you read my various stories, you will learn just how important my digging skill is. The applications are virtually endless.

Just imagine you want to hide something or uncover something... or dig a hole in which to plant something... or just to dig because it's so much fun! Man, all that dirt flying is really cool. I've never gotten a true measurement in altitude, but that stuff can fly pretty dog-gone high!

Okay... I've also tracked a LOT of dirt indoors... and I mean a LOT!!! Oh yeah, I've been banished from the house for life more than once. (Hah! And cats thought <u>they</u> were the only ones with nine lives.)

I can't say that my humans are properly impressed with my prowess yet. However, I am working on them! More on my digging is coming up. Meanwhile, there's nothing like a long rest on the cool grass after a big dig!

Wow! My Labrador Retriever side really shows when I'm furless!

9
MY OWN APARTMENT

If you are a host to your guest, be a host to his dog also.
--Russian Proverb

Some dogs have doghouses and even kennels. I've tried those, but I just couldn't seem to find something I really liked. I even tried an igloo once, but it just wasn't "me."

My Miss Nina went inside, and she looked as cute as can be. I still didn't care for it. I mean, how would you decorate an igloo? Although, I admit, I really liked the carpeting; so, I kept the floor liner for my bed.

Anyway, I basically live in the human house. You know, they let me in and let me out and let me in and let me out. (It gives them regular exercise, which humans really need.) However, during the daytime, when they aren't home, I actually have my own place. My very own apartment.

It wasn't exactly turn-key; it needed a lot of work. Still, it's all mine! My very own digs. (Hah! No pun intended.) And it's got a great location, too. Location, location, location. (I even got it without paying a real estate commission!)

You see, my humans have this really big sunroom porch that's up high. And there's nothing but space underneath. Well, they actually had tried to store a couple ladders and some gardening equipment there. But, hah! I just put a little oomph behind it, and I moved that stuff aside! Remember... the digging skill is very important!

Initially, I dug one room. Then I was ready to expand. You know, I thought it would be nice to have different rooms for different moods or weather days. When I started my expansion, my humans thought someone was breaking in.

Nahhhh, I'd never allow that! I was merely, uhhhh, rearranging the "furniture" to clear space to dig another room. Yeaaaah, that's it.

I've since expanded once again, so my apartment now has not just two, but three rooms. My humans actually call them "nests." But do I look like some fine-feathered bird?!? No, I don't think so. These rooms stay so nice and cool all summer. Yeah... air-conditioning... no extra charge! And there I am, as snug as a bug in a rug.

It's great having room to invite friends! You never know when a four-legged buddy might come calling. It's good to be ready. Mr. Hospitality here! Hah!

The location is perfect for knowing when folks come and go, too. I can hear everything. So, I hear my humans as they drive into the yard. I come running, but they always seem to know when I've been enlarging or re-arranging my apartment. Hmmmm... they say that the sand on my nose and face gives me away every time. Hee hee.

10
FOUR-LEGGED FRIENDS

A dog is a smile and a wagging tail.
What is between them doesn't matter much.
                              --Clara Ortega, Writer

In my puppy days, I grew up with a dog named Cocoa and a cat named Maestro. They showed me the ropes of learning the neighborhood and even hunting. That was back when I was a New Yorker and starting life on Long Island.

Of course, that was just after I'd been an orphan pup. Wow, did I get lucky! It sure was great getting some solid training as a youngin'… to get started on the right track, and all that. Then, POW! Within just a couple of years, I had moved to New Hampshire, where a whole wonderful new world surrounds me… and lots of new furry friends.

Sir Winston

My first friend was a little English Cocker Spaniel named Sir Winston. He was a really good guy, but we had a rather bad start.

That's me with my buddy Winston!

You see, I came around the corner of my house and there he was growling and rolling around on the ground on top of my Cathy human. I hadn't met Winston yet, and I thought this beast was attacking my Cathy. She was growling right back. Yikes... this scene was like a bag of cats! I knew I'd better get in there and protect her. NO dog can attack my humans and get away with it! I was taking him OUT. No hesitation. I lunged at full speed.

Suddenly, there was my own Big Dog (The Ronald), literally catching me mid-air. Oops! Good thing. Turns out Winston was meant to be a buddy. He and my Cathy were just playing. She'd known him for years. (She called him Winstonian.) They'd played like that forever... "rough and tumble" she calls it, with lots of rolling around and growling.

Whew! That was close. And she was right. Winston was only about 26 pounds, but he became a good buddy. I just wish I could have known him longer before he went to Doggie Heaven. (I'll catch up with him later.)

Vivi

Then along came the definition of miniature rug rat. She showed up with my Cathy human's brother, Jim. He says Vivi is a dog, but I would have bet my last biscuit that she is really just a very skinny squirrel that barks. Her name is Olivia, and Olive for short, but everyone calls her Vivi.

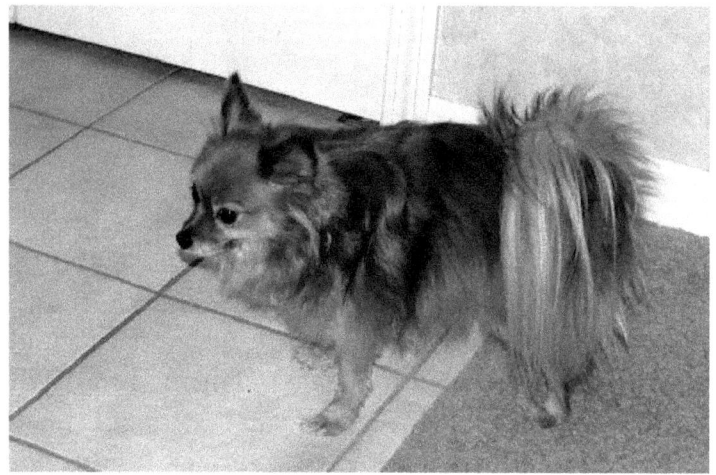

Olivia... (a.k.a. Vivi) on a visit to see me

She is reportedly a mini Pomeranian, but Vivi tells me that she's actually a reeeally small Rotweiler. (She was a rescue, too, so there may be confusion.) She also may be a tree-dwelling type dog because she mostly hangs out on Jim's shoulder.

Sometimes she leaves her bird's-eye view perch and gets on the ground with me. She then barks like mad. Goodness gracious, Vivi... don't have kittens for crying out loud!!

I don't think I should get too close when she does this. Since she only weighs about 2-1/2 to 3 pounds, she could get caught between my toes!

Vivi only eats three or four crunchy bits as a whole meal. Man, I'd feel cheated if someone tried to give me <u>that</u> little as even just a treat. Jeez... I <u>spill</u> more than that on the floor when I eat!

Anyway, Vivi really looks and moves like a squirrel, but she sounds like a soprano dog. She is quite a marvel. Hey, because she spends most of the time perching on her human's shoulder, maybe she really is some new kind of furry bird!

<u>Gringus</u>

I met another dog owned by Miss Nina's older sister, Keira. This dog's name was Danza, but then he became Gringus. (I think he chose that name because he liked it better.)

Gringus playing

He was a little tough at first... like a bear with a sore head. Hey, those Brooklyn city streets will do that to a young guy! So, I understood that he has no respect for my humans' house and couldn't even understand basic lingo like, "No."

It's good that Keira rescued that pup. She helped him have a great life. He seems like a good guy – just a little rough around the edges. He simply needs a little direction and discipline and a whole lot of love.

Keira gave him plenty of that. And her big brother, Christopher, even taught Gringus to like cats. Well, actually it was probably Christopher's cat that taught Gringus. Yup, good ole' Skelator to the rescue! Oh, and Keira's cat, Monster, too!

Gringus and Monster

Later on, Gringus was ready to be adopted… the same way I was. He came to live with me for a little while he waited for his adoption.

Man, I knew he'd have no trouble finding a home. He's so talented! You should hear him sing. Truly! I'll bet he's loving life in his new home. No more city streets for him... he's gone country. Yee-Haw!

Shyla

Next came an amazing chick into my life. (Ooh, sorry if that's not politically correct, but I'm busy swooning.) Her name is Shyla, but she is not shy. She IS a true beauty by anyone's definition. She is my best girl... it was puppy love at first sight.

Shyla has two different colored eyes, which I hear is a Husky tradition. Seriously. Her left one is brown and her right one is bright blue. It's awesome. All I know is that the second I saw her, I was ready to show her my etchings. (Hmmmm, what are etchings, anyway?!?)

Shyla... my all-time favorite babe... I mean dog!

I immediately toured her all around my yard and took her to see some of my favorite places, like my brook. She loved it. Shyla is the first dog I ever invited to my apartment. (I'm sure she was impressed that I have my very own place, as well as living in the human's house.)

She was my date for a big barbecue my humans had. Shyla and I ran all around and had a blast. Then we just flopped down in the middle of the partygoers so they could all "ooh" and "ah" over us. They were cool and just stepped over us, and not on us. (Actually they also said that I am the thickest bear rug they'd ever seen! Hah!)

Anyway, back to my Shyla. We romp and play. She is a very independent woman, but when she's visiting my house, she is all mine.

We've also spent some time on my humans' boat. I always try to be a perfect gentleman for Shyla. I let her drink from my water dish. I even stand back and let her have a drink first. (Hey, I know the humans will refill it as often as we need.)

Once I had to be a bit protective. Shyla was coming to spend the day with me on the boat, but another guy came by the dock. You know the type. He was a real long-haired, golden boy – yeah, the retriever type. Probably a surfer dude or something.

Well, he came right over after Shyla. (I suspect that they'd shared a water bowl or two in the past.) He and I barked at each other, but I wasn't backing down. SHE was spending that day with ME! Hah! Miles wins again!

Bandit

Then came the little baby boy, Bandit, born on Thanksgiving, 2004 at the Best of Breed Puppy Ranch in Zephyr Hills, Florida. He always comes visiting with my Grammy and Grand Poppy Burnham. They say he'll never grow larger than 7 pounds. Wow! That's like one of my paws! (Actually, I'm not sure, but I think I eat that much for lunch.)

His photos make him look much bigger than he really is. Believe me, it's all fluff and fur. If you saw him soaking wet, you'd be hard-pressed to ever believe the 7 pounds! He looks *tiny* underneath all that fluffiness.

Bandit with Grand Poppy & Grammy Burnham on Big Dog's boat

Bandit is a Maltipoo, which I'm told means he's half Maltese and half Poodle. He's actually a pretty scrappy fella for such a little munchkin. He'll literally zip in and steal my huge rawhide bone, right out of my mouth. That's gutsy. I like that. I'm truly a gentle giant, but he didn't know that at first.

To tell you the truth, Bandit has wayyyyy too much energy. I get dog-tired just watching him! He's very young, of course. So, he hasn't learned yet how nice it is just to flop down on the floor at the humans' feet and relax. Oh, no. Not Bandit! He's full of "vim and vinegar." You know – go, go, go energy! He probably shouldn't drink coffee or anything else with caffeine. Can you imagine!!!

Well, someday he'll figure out how great napping is. For now, he seems to have made it his personal mission to keep me young. Hah! Can you tell that I'm smiling? We are best friends... #1 buddies!

I've had a number of other good buddies over the years, too. That's just one of many aspects of my life that make me one lucky dog. Some I have gotten to know well... some I've barely met, but I hear my humans talk about them, so I feel as though I know them well, too.

Daisy with Grandma Martin

There's Daisy who lives on a farm with my Grandma and Grandpa (BeBop) Martin in North Carolina.

Big Dog with Grandma & BeBop Martin
(BeBop is Nina-speak for Grandpa!)

Oh, and Charlie, who lives in Manchester, NH in the winters and on Paugus Bay at Lake Winnipesaukee in the summers.

Charlie, who cares for his humans, the Gamache family

And you'd just love the guys I call the M&Ms. No, they're not chocolate. But their names are Max and Murray.

Murray weighs about 16 pounds, though he's a Maltipoo. I think I'd have to describe Murray as a soft bundle of love.

Murray and his mom, Ashley

Max, on the other hand, is teeny-weeny on the outside, because he's a little terrier. But don't you dare tell him that he's not a purebred Labrador Retriever.

Can't keep him out of the water. He can fetch so many times in a row even I lose count. He's quite a workout for his humans.

Oh, and if someone splashes, he thinks it's his job to defend against the water. He literally tries to bite the beads of water. He's fun to watch.

Max enjoying the sunshine

They now live in Texas with their humans Ashley and Chris, but they used to spend their summers on the boat right beside my humans' boat.

Sigh... so many buddies... so little time.

11
MY TURF

A door is what a dog is perpetually on the wrong side of.
     --Ogden Nash, American Poet (1902-1971)

You really should see my turf. It's the greatest. I regularly patrol the borders. That keeps me as busy as a beaver.

Sometimes it means sloshing in my brook, uncovering a turtle or two. Or you might find me trotting along this long stonewall we have out front. I like that place. There's always a chipmunk or two that wants to play hide-and-seek. Boy, am I good at finding them! I can't hide well when it's my turn though. I don't understand it because I sit so perfectly still. Oh well. I am very good at seeking and finding the chipmunks.

I either sit quietly, just like my first cat taught me, and I wait patiently for the chipmunk to pop back out of whatever hole he chose for hiding. Or, if I'm feeling impatient, I just dive right into the stonewall and find them! Oh yeahhhh... it's the great digging skill working for me again. (Oh, just let me know if you need any stonewalls taken down; I'm very good at it.)

Me… patrolling my back yard

I also like patrolling the woods. I find all sorts of playthings. Among my humans' favorites are the snakes. They usually let me play on my own with the critters that I find, but they really get excited when I waltz up to them with snakes.

I proudly bring that writhing toy onto the lawn, flipping it all around, and my humans come running to join in, carrying a rake or some such thing. Yeah, they take my snake away from me. They usually just fling it back into the woods.

Hah! I can play fetch in the woods just as easily as on the lawn, so I bring that snake right back to them.

Humans don't seem to have good staying power at this game. Pretty soon they are tired and start telling me <u>not</u> to fetch the snake.

Inspecting the new raised rose garden

Of course, when I'm not playing or romping in the woods, I patrol the areas where my humans can see me too, like along the flowerbeds. I like them to know that I'm always on duty doing my rounds and guarding the perimeter... the Ever-Ready Bunny of Bowzers!

12
SQUIRREL PATROL

If your dog is fat, you aren't getting enough exercise.
--Anonymous

Keeping the rodents at bay is one of my favorite activities. I watch them from my window. Those squirrels can be very brazen. They come right up on our deck and climb onto the railing. Then they try to leap through the air onto the bird feeders. They usually fail, and that's the <u>most</u> fun to watch. They can entertain me all day with their pointless antics.

My humans even helped me torment them by hanging a special bird feeder designed to spin around and toss the squirrels off if they try to stand on the bird's perches. And they hung this feeder in easy range for the squirrels. Now THAT is really fun to watch. And those pesky squirrels don't seem very smart... they don't catch on at all. Hah! Monkey see, monkey do. And they do it over and over again!

Every once in a while, the squirrels do make a totally spectacular leap and land on one of the regular feeders. Then, of course, they start munching. Left to their own devices, they would just sit there and eat all my birdies' food, so I have to get rid of them.

If I'm inside, my humans help me sneak up on the squirrels. They whisper, "Squirrels." I leap up, but then immediately switch into M.S.M., which stands for Miles' Stealth Mode. That means I don't woof a single word, and I slowly approach on tippy toes. (It's true… I've truly learned to tip toe.) Then my humans quietly slide open the back door. And, in a flash, I'm off… dashing across the deck and into the yard! Squirrels are flying through the air trying to get to safety. I guess they're flying squirrels.

I usually get them stuck up a tree. They chatter angrily at me, and I bark right back at them. Hah! Sneaking is fun!

I have another great technique. If I'm already outside or my humans let me out the front door, I zip around to the backyard at full speed. By the time those pesky squirrels see me coming, it's too late. Wow! Now I'm at full speed heading right for 'em.

I <u>love</u> squirrel patrol. But just as soon as I drive them out, new squirrels seem to find my haven and move in. It's an ongoing battle. But this is a task I take very seriously. You see, we had a squirrel invasion once.

My Cathy human had been told that if you feed the squirrels in their <u>own</u> feeders, they'll leave the <u>bird</u> feeders alone. Sounds reasonable. She kept a huge bin of peanuts for the squirrels and regularly filled their boxes outside for them.

This worked great until this one time when we were all away on vacation for a few days. Though she left plenty of extra peanuts outside for the squirrels, they were real pigs and took advantage of my absence.

The squirrels literally threw a HUGE party on our screened-in porch. No, I'm totally serious. They chewed several big squirrel doors through the screens and then even chewed a hole into the peanut bin.

Oh man, my humans were annoyed when we got home. These squirrel partygoers never even picked up after themselves. There were peanut shells all over the porch. Shells covered every table and chair, every corner, every floorboard, and every railing. It was one wild party, you could tell.

My Big Dog said he thought that Budweiser had probably been here filming a commercial. We could picture all those fat squirrels hanging out on all the furniture, eating peanuts and drinking beer amidst lots of loud music. Parrrrtyyyy!

Well, that was it. No more feeding the squirrels. My humans actually got this Have-A-Heart trap. Within a week, I'd helped Big Dog take away more than two-dozen squirrels. I knew from that moment on that squirrel control was a very important way in which I could help my humans. I am vigilant in my duties. I never again have permitted gangs of squirrels. Hah! Not in *my* "hood." Not on *my* watch. In fact, I try to keep it to a maximum of two squirrels in the area.

If I slip, and one day there are three, Big Dog reminds me that I'm slackin' on my Squirrel Detail. I spring right into action and drop those numbers to zero as fast as I can. (Just between us dogs, but this is not work at all. So, please don't tell my humans that it's reeeeeally fun!!)

13
DUCK FLUSHING

The *dog was created especially for children.*
He is the god of frolic.
--Henry Ward Beecher, American Clergyman (1813-1887)

One of my favorite border patrol areas is the part with a big pond. I especially like it when the ducks don't hear me coming. Yup, I wait until I've got my ducks all in a row. Then I spring into action, bounding boing, boing, boing, splash, as I join them in the water.

What fun! You should see all my ducks quacking and squawking as they fly up into the sky. I'm definitely the rooster in the henhouse. They are not impressed with my entrance. Hah!

If they didn't have such little birdbrains, they'd probably figure out that I hear them chattering with each other. It reminds me that they're there... it also invites me to come and play! However, in my pond is not the only place I get to play with the ducks.

Every Spring I look forward to the ducks and geese flying north again. Many of them make nests near my house! There's this big wooded hill with a brook, and they really seem to like it there. I wait for them to all get settled on their nests, real quiet-like. Then I come leaping gleefully in. Wow! You should see the feathers fly. They make such a wonderful ruckus. I just giggle and gallop away... until next time. They truly are among my favorite fine-feathered friends.

My Nina likes them too, but she prefers to feed them. But I'll admit, I've known her to stand on the end of the boat, entice them close with cheese puffs and crackers and then... POW... she jumps into the water with them. They scatter noisily. Ha-ha-ha! She must have seen me playing with the ducks and knew instantly that flushing the ducks would be fun.

Nina feeding the ducks

Now, let's get back to me bounding into the woods after the nesting ducks. When I tell you that I bound... boing, boing, boing, I should really explain.

My humans say that I look like a huge cartoon deer. From a full run or a standing position, I can instantly shift into bounding mode.

This means that I spring from all four feet high into the air; my knees hardly bend. It usually only takes me three or four "boings" to leave the yard and be well into the woods. It works very effectively, though it most assuredly makes the humans laugh out loud.

14
BIRD DOG

It's no coincidence that man's best friend cannot talk.
                                                          --Anonymous

Birds are so cool. I can sit and watch them for hours. In fact, I do, but I'm as wise as an owl about it. I sit sooo still. I try not to blink or twitch an ear or even a whisker. Then the birdies don't see me. Remember, I'm the original Stealth Dog!

Hah! The birdies get pretty comfortable and eventually come down to the ground. From out of nowhere, I pounce! They usually fly away, as free as birds. But they really scold me like mad for startling them. Hee hee. They're good play buddies.

Now I've already told you about my duck flushing expertise. You probably don't yet know how good I am at getting the sneakier birds, like Ruffed Grouse. I am very patient. And I've learned a wonderful trick. It's hard for me to tiptoe silently in the woods. So, I listen to the rustling of the birds in the woods, and I follow those sounds, keeping my toes on the grass along the edge. I really can be silent as a mouse, and they don't know I'm tracking them! (Now you know one Miles Secret!)

I remember this one grouse that just wasn't thinking straight. Crazy as a loon, quite frankly. I guess it had spent a couple of days trying to scare my Cathy human out of our own yard. Yeah, right! Like that's going to happen!

Seriously. One day I saw my Cathy human pulling some weeds in a flowerbed by the driveway. I started trotting over to visit. But, wait just a minute! There was that angry grouse heading straight for her from another direction. Attack one of MY humans, will you!?!

Well, when that grouse saw me, it scurried into the brush in the woods lickety-split. That ruffed grouse could sneak super low under a lot of the brush.

Hah! Remember, I know the secret. I just listened to those little grousy footsteps and began biding my time. As I crept along the edge of the woods, the grouse didn't even know I was there.

Suddenly, I pounced, bounding lithely into the woods. Okay, I missed on my first couple of attempts. But I am patient. Within minutes, I had my catch and carried it proudly out of the woods to my surprised humans. They really shouldn't be surprised. I'm very good at this sort of thing.

Actually, I almost caught a really tall bird they told me is called a Great Blue Heron. My humans said that I have to give this bird a break. He's on some list of endangered species or something.

Okay, so I can't catch him, but that doesn't mean I'm just gonna let him walk around in my yard and eat my goldfish and bull frogs. No way.

He tries to stand very still, so he looks like a pond statue or a spindly tree or something. But I can see him. I bark very loudly whenever I catch him in my yard. And I chase him away. Yeah, he's smarter than the ruffed grouse. He flies away. I can't do that… yet.

This year I'll focus on another bird I've been watching. They say it's called a pheasant. Hmmmm. It's rather pretty. Maybe I'll just keep watching it for a while.

There are some other feathered freaks that I'm told are birds, but I don't really think so. They are really quite ugly. Real turkeys to be exact.

Oh, I'm serious. These don't look like the turkeys I see in the pictures – all plump and brown with a big fan of tail feathers. No! These are tall and gangly, gray and wrinkly, with skinny little heads. Okay, sometimes they fan out their tail feathers, but usually they just look strange.

Turkeys in my yard!

They visit in big groups. Sometimes there are just six or eight, but at other times they really have a party. I've seen two or three dozen drop by just to see if my birdies spilled any food on the ground under the feeders. Yup, these turkeys are scavengers.

They don't sing any pretty songs either, unlike most of my feathered friends. They're just constantly gobble-gobbling amongst themselves. A little birdie told me that they call it "talking turkey." Whatever.

If you want to laugh out loud, you should see them try and fly! They sort of lumber along like overloaded troop transport planes that appear to barely be able to lift off the ground. They just look goofy!

I fear that is what I'd look like if I tried to fly, so I just watch. If there's anything I don't want to do, it's look as goofy as these turkeys look.

I hear it said that turkeys make for some good eating. At least that's what the humans say. Well, I'm not going to try it. They can eat these silly looking birds if they want to. I guess the humans just haven't heard the old adage, "You are what you eat!"

Now, if you're into history, you probably also know that an early human in this country, a man named Benjamin Franklin, wanted to have the turkey deemed as the national bird. Ohhhh, that would have been embarrassing in this day and age. I mean I've seen eagles too, and they were a much more dignified choice.

In fact, once I got to watch a Mama Eagle teaching her Baby Eagle how to catch this thermal lift thing up in the sky. Mama got flying in a small circle and was going higher and higher, with Baby right behind her.

Now and then, Baby would lose it and fall out of the up draft. Mama Eagle just swooped back to her chick and got him back on track. Finally the little fella really got it, and I watched the two of them fly in that circle up, up, up until I couldn't even see them. Wow… that *is* the champion of birds.

15
FISH STORIES

*If dogs could talk
it would take a lot of the fun out of owning one.*
--Andrew Aitken "Andy" Rooney,
American Journalist & Commentator (1919 - 2011)

Fishing is a fun sport. My humans built this great little pond and waterfall by our house. They don't like me messin' with the flowers there though. Yeahhhh, I got in trouble a couple of times for digging there. But how could I help it? Ponds are pretty irresistible.

My little buddy, Bandit, had never seen a pond before visiting me. He's the little Maltipoo I told you about earlier. Wow, did he get a surprise when he went to the pond the first time! I guess he thought he could just walk across the pond lilies and such. He got an unplanned bath instead.

I know that Bandit is a real lightweight and all that, but I had to explain to him that he's a whole lot bigger than a frog, which is the lily's maximum weight load. (We got Bandit a little life jacket after that... just in case he ever tries to walk on water again.)

Anyway, this particular pond that my humans built also grows these really cool, bright orange fish. I look into the water, and they come to the surface and look back at me. Well, without a net, what could I do?

The first time I saw them, I just grabbed one in my mouth. Yum! They are great! This probably means that I like sushi, but please hold the rice. Oh, and no wasabi for me, please. It makes me sneeze.

Anyway, I guess my humans weren't very impressed with my new taste for fish. I tried to share one with my Cathy human. When I put it into her hand, she screamed.

Hey, it was as clean as a hound's tooth, but I guess she hadn't realized that I'd already eaten half of it... you know... as a taste test to be sure it was safe for her first. You can never be too careful with fresh food. (Hey, I've eaten a couple of bad road kills, so I know! I was as sick as a dog.)

Anyway, they don't let me fish in that pond any more. They actually covered the top with all this water lettuce stuff, so I can't see the fish.

I faked them out. I found another spot for fishing. We've got a babbling brook behind our house. It's really cool. The deer share it with me. That's very nice of them.

I can walk right into the water. It's crystal clear and cool and bubbles all around my legs right up to my belly. When I see something that I need to check out "up close and personal," I just poke my face under the water and grab it!

Frog inspection

Fish, frogs, turtles – you name it. Now, I'm not fishing for a compliment here, but I'm pretty good. But I've stopped sharing my catch with my humans. They just tend to say things like, "Eeeeywwwww!" (I don't know how to spell that, but it sounds pretty weird when they say it.)

Anyway, the brook is another of my favorite places. Oh, and I'll be a monkey's uncle… in the winter I can even walk straight across on top of it without even getting wet, but it is very slippery. Heck, even little Bandit wouldn't need a life jacket!

16

ON THE RECORD

Dogs love their friends and bite their enemies,
quite unlike people, who are incapable of pure love
and always have to mix love and hate.
--Sigmund Freud, Austrian Psychologist (1856-1939)

I learned that there is this thing called a Leash Law. It means that I'm supposed to not wander freely through the neighborhood. Well, I pretty much stay in my yard... except when some critter races away from me across the street... or I hear the ducks chattering away down over the hill... or there are horses or people I need to go meet out on the street.

One day, during my first summer in New Hampshire, my poor Cathy human was so distraught. She heard the squealing tires of someone trying to break hard to avoid hitting me. Oooops. The pavement was so warm that I'd stretched out for a nap. Bad time for that motorcycle to be coming along... he was about to hit one big, furry speed bump.

He stopped in time. I got up. He started to go around me, and I did what any dog worth his salt would do... I started to bite at his tires. Oh, and bark very loudly.

My Cathy human was horrified. Turns out it was a policeman on a motorcycle. (She was not impressed with me.) She called out to me very sternly. I ran right to her and she immediately started taking me back to this big kennel they'd made for me.

We didn't get there. The policeman turned around and came into the driveway to talk with us. Oh-oh... I'm busted.

You see, after Big Dog made my kennel, I chewed my way out to show him that I didn't like it. Yup... strong as an ox... I gnawed off the parts holding the walls together. Pretty smart, huh? Well, they kept trying different things to keep me in, but I'm quite an escape artist... must have some Pooch-dini in me.

Everyone is also very impressed at how I manage to sneak into some places. For example, we had a family of bunny rabbits move in under the back deck.

Okay. Okay. That's too low for me to fit underneath. But when those little bunnies hopped under the boards, I simply HAD to scamper in after them.

Hmmmm... perhaps scamper is not the right word. My Cathy human actually described my technique as the G.I. Joe belly crawl. I'd just flatten myself out as much as possible and sort of wriggle my way over the crushed rock under the decking. It wasn't very speedy, but I'd get in there. Those "wacky wabbits," however, did not want to play with me. They'd hop away from me just as I'd start to get close.

Big Dog finally blocked off the one place through which I could get under the deck, so my days doing the G.I. Joe belly crawl are over. They said I was honorably discharged and thanked me for my service.

Anyway, back to my legal beagle story… the police officer didn't take me to jail or give me a ticket. I was lucky. Turns out his wife and my Cathy human are friends. Wow. That was close! They also had a dog at home and were having the same I-don't-want-to-stay-in-a-cage challenge with their dog. So, I was forgiven, but I learned that I better stay in my own yard… or else!

I did have one other run-in with The Law. We were all outside working by the stonewall… you know, raking up dried leaves and stuff. A strange man rode up on a bicycle. I barked at him and he started yelling at my Cathy human… I mean a LOT.

She called me to her, and I ran right over to her side. Unfortunately, this Bike Man didn't leave. He came right up to her screaming in her face. Oooooh… he was nasty… meaner than a junkyard dog. She was scared. I did NOT like this one little bit. I got right between them to protect her. Hah! I barked even louder than he was yelling. They say that a barking dog never bites, but this guy was pushing my limits pretty hard.

Even Big Dog was alerted and came right over. Between Big Dog and the Miles-Mannered Man, ol' Bike Man finally figured he better ride away. But he was not very nice; he said he was going straight to the police.

Yup. Pretty soon a big cruiser pulled into the yard. Big Dog and my Cathy human told the officer what had happened. He then wanted to see the vicious dog that Bike Man had reported. Oh, oh! Now, I'm _really_ busted. I can't exactly pretend to be a goldfish!

So, I dutifully trotted over to his feet, flopped down, rolled over and bared my belly. I mean what else could I do under the circumstances? Might as well throw myself on his mercy.

He liked me. He could instantly see that while I will protect my humans if they are threatened, I am really as gentle as a lamb.

The policeman must have realized that I'm a great guy, because I didn't even get a ticket. (But I do admit that I'm glad Bike Man has never returned… I gave him a warning, and he was smart enough to heed it.)

17
TOYS AND TREATS

*If a dog's prayers were answered,
bones would rain from the sky.*

--Proverb

I have some of the greatest toys and goodies you could imagine! My favorite is a red rubber globe with a little hole in it. My Cathy human loads it up with goodies that fall out one by one as I roll the ball around with my nose.

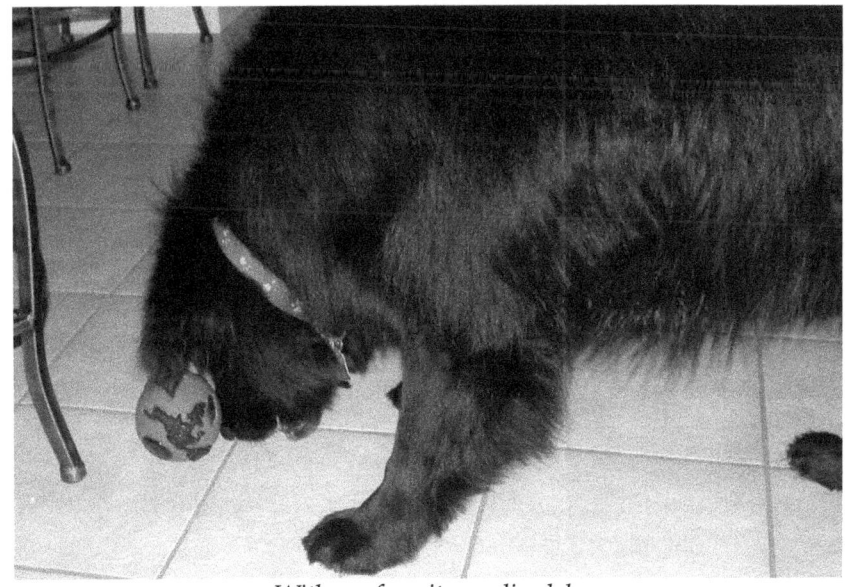

With my favorite goodie globe

She tries to pretend she puts vitamins and healthy things inside, but she can't fool me. It's just full of treats. I love that thing! I've gotten really good at fishing it back out from under low things like chairs, where it tries to escape from me and gets stuck.

I've got other toys, too. There's this one big furry purple thing that the humans throw, and I bring it back to them. I shake it a lot while it's in my mouth, but I don't want to hurt it. That's because I think there must be a very small kid inside.

It's true; I hear laughter inside when my humans toss it. They try to tell me it's just a laughing box, but I'm not so sure.

One other favorite of mine is a giant rawhide bone. The humans don't let me take it outside, probably because I'll bury it. But I carry it around with me inside the house.

Now, my humans would tell you that I whine and whimper and cry over it for about three weeks before I eat it, but I'm just talking to it, really.

Or maybe what they hear is the rawhide bone. It thinks it's my baby and it cries because it misses me and wants to remind me not to leave it alone again. Yeah, that's it.

When I go upstairs with my humans to watch a movie or to escape a thunderstorm, I usually figure out fast that I've left my big rawhide bone in the kitchen. I scurry off and bring it right back.

It's true that after about three weeks, I start to eat it. But I try to make it last as long as possible. That's not easy!

Hah! You should see Big Dog with my rawhide bone. He thinks it's a soccer ball, so he kicks it away from me across the floor.

Well he can do all the hot-dogging he wants, but can he outfox the Miles? Yahhhh – when pigs fly! I <u>always</u> get it right back.

Anyway, during all the days of devouring, you will find me still carrying my rawhide bone with me. Nahhhh, it's not a security blanket thing at all. I just don't want it to get lonely.

18
DOG OF THE YEAR

The cat is mighty dignified until the dog comes by.
--Southern US Folk Saying

I've always liked cats, and they've always liked me, too. That is, until I met these chubby black ones with white stripes down their backs. They just don't care for me at all, and they've got the nastiest way of letting me know it! Gross!

This striped black and white beauty wouldn't even talk to me the first time we met. It just zapped me with this absolutely foul-smelling spray.

By morning I had the whole house smelling rotten. Yup. I'd been skunked. My humans were not impressed. They kept bathing me in tomato juice and vinegar and stuff like that.

I swear it took months before I smelled like my ol' self again. But I learned.

Okay... I didn't learn right away. I guess that I needed another lesson just to be sure that first encounter wasn't a fluke.

Now, let me give you a little background to set the stage. You see, there's this great Newfy named Josh. I think he is the first Newfoundland to win "Best in Show" / "Dog of the Year" at the big Westminster Kennel Club dog show. I sometimes watch that with my humans. (I don't care much for the itsy-bitsy, fluffer-nutter, little dust mop type dogs. It's the big Working Class dogs that I like to see!)

Anyway, shortly after Josh made us all as proud as peacocks in 2004, rising from the Working Class to become the Number One dog in the world, I had a little accident. Yeah, my second run in with a stinky cat. I got skunked! Again! (You think I'd have learned to look out for that white stripe down its back, but I kept thinking that they'd figure out that I'm a really good buddy. Nope!)

Anyway, one night there it was... this big black kitty with the long white stripe... just sitting under Big Dog's car. I tried to say, "Hi," but it sprayed me mercilessly, right in the face! This was the absolute worst! I couldn't get away from myself.

My humans took me to some groomers who had to shave off all my gorgeous long hair... yeahhh, right down to the skin. Naked as a jaybird! Well, they actually left my tail intact.

I realize that they were only trying to help, but it made me look pretty goofy. And exposed! Big Dog's friends told him that he ought to put some pants on me. Seriously?

The worst part was that I didn't look like a dog any more. My face still looked like a dog, but between my long flowing tail and the shaved body fur, everyone said I looked like a pony with a dog's face. Scheeeeez! How ridiculous! (Not to mention chilly!!!)

Okay, already... take a picture. It lasts longer.

Wow, I never even knew what cold was before <u>that</u> Spring. Yikes! Cold nose, warm heart – my foot! I was freezing inside and out! I'd run outside and do my business and then zoooom back to the door soooo fast!! Come on, Summer!

Mostly, it was just embarrassing. I mean, I'm supposed to look like Josh – gorgeous and full-bodied with LOTS of great fluffy long fur. Dog of the Year. Best in Show. Riiiiight. I didn't even look related! Just for a viable excuse, I actually started telling people that I was in the Witness Protection Program. Bad scene.

I've cleverly avoided the white-striped black kitties since then. Yeah. Good idea!

19
PRICKLY KITTIES

A dog believes you are what you think you are.
  --Jane Ellen Swan, American Author (1925-2010)

Speaking of strange cats, I almost forgot to tell you about some very pointed critters I've met. (I think I was trying to block the memory from my mind.) I just don't understand them at all. They look sort of like chubby kitties, but they walk funny. They lumber and roll along. I think their legs must be too short.

They've got some angry bees in their bonnet; I think they're either self-conscious or angry that they don't have nice, soft, fine fur like other critters. They've got horrid needles where fur is supposed to be. They are as prickly as a porcupine. Hah! Just try to get to know one; you'll learn fast that they are just plain rude.

Man, I'd only been at my new home in New Hampshire for about an hour when I met my first one. All I did was give it a little tiny nudge with my nose – you know, to say, "Hi!"

Maybe it was in a cranky mood; I don't know. But it shot all these little spears into my face. A quilling experience, to say the least! I ran back to my new house. I was frantic.

My Big Dog Ron sent the Cathy human to get something to use to remove the quills. Good, because they hurt! She came right back fast with tweezers. Big Dog laughed at her and had her get pliers, which are like giant tweezers.

Then I had to sit really still while he pulled them out. OUCH! But I knew he was trying to help me; I knew right from the start that I could trust him. Sure enough, very soon I was free of quills. Then, ohhhhh, it felt soooo good to dive my nose into my nice cool water dish! Ahhhh.

Quilling Revisited

You might logically think that one exciting experience with a porcupine would teach me to leave these critters alone. Awwww, but I like critters, and I'm sure they'd like me too... if only they'd give me a chance. Okay, so I'm downright bull-headed.

A couple years after my first encounter, I got a perfect chance to make a positive difference in dog-porcupine relations. I saw a little baby pinecone "kitty." Surely this little tyke hadn't yet been taught to hate me! So, I gently moved in to say hello. Wrong again, Miles!

Yikes!!! This little baby porcupine filled my whole face with many dozens of baby-fine quills. Wow! They are just wayyyy too willing to "share!" I made a beeline for home, but my humans didn't come back for an hour or so. Wow, I was anxiously awaiting their return!

Because these quills were so young and delicate, I managed to break a bunch of them off by rubbing my chin on the driveway. Turns out that wasn't such a smart idea, because the portion still below my skin really hurt.

Even my Big Dog couldn't pull all these little quills out. He tried his best, but it was horrible. It was late at night, and Big Dog and my Cathy human rushed me to the doggie hospital. I don't remember much; I must have taken a nap. It's a good thing the doctor could work and just let this sleeping dog lie, because he managed to get every single quill removed before I even woke up! And there were my humans to greet me.

Woaaaah! I think I must have been drugged or something. I swear I could see two Cathy humans and two Big Dogs. I couldn't even walk straight, so all four of my Ron and Cathy humans (maybe more), helped me into the back of my SUV and took me home.

Actually, I couldn't sit up without tipping over, so the two Cathy humans sat with me in my way back section and held onto me the whole way home. That was nice.

The morale of this story is, "If it looks like a porcupine and it waddles like a porcupine, get the point without getting the points!!!"

20
STEALTH MODE

Only mad dogs and Englishmen go out in the noonday sun.
--Indian Proverb

I am sure the "Pink Panther" theme music was playing the night I sneaked into a Marriott Hotel. Since I'm not usually the sneaky type, let me explain.

My humans drove to Long Island in New York. I was so excited because I got to go, too. But the trip was long, and they were too tired to drive back home. So, they decided to stay at a hotel. Oh-oh! Surely Mr. Marriott did not want such a furry guest as I am.

Big Dog had often joked about plans to dress me in a big trench coat, turn up the collar, and cover my head with a hat, tilted down to hide my face. He said my humans would then help me walk through a hotel lobby on just my back feet. They said they would just pretend I was a very drunk friend they were helping to the room. Oh, my! Was this the night?

Phew... that was just talk. I tried to tell them that I could sleep comfortably in the back of our car. They thought it might get too cold for me overnight. Helloooo! Newfy!

Anyway, their room in the hotel was on the fourth floor. My Cathy human propped opened the room door and stood watch outside the elevator on the fourth floor. She then called my Nina on a cell phone and told her to open the first floor back door to the parking lot right across from the downstairs elevator. Big Dog was standing with me outside, just waiting for the signal. Suddenly, there it was! The door cracked open.

My Nina and Big Dog were whispering, so I knew I needed to be very quiet, too. I learned this routine from all my squirrel chasing episodes. So, I tip-toed as gingerly as possible across the hallway and into the elevator. Thank goodness for my nimble-footed dexterity!

I guess my stealth posture caught my humans by surprise, however. My Nina and Big Dog started laughing so hard in the elevator that Cathy said she could hear them all the way up on the fourth floor. Oh, well.

Finally, the elevator door opened on the fourth floor. There was my Cathy human, motioning for me to come. She started whispering to all of us, "Shhhhhh!"

I first peered out of the elevator, very carefully looking both directions to be sure the coast was clear. I'd come too far to risk getting caught and kicked out now! On tippy-toes, I crouched low and dashed around the corner, across the hall, and through the open door to safety.

Then I sprawled out on the floor beside one of the beds where no one would see me. Cathy and I waited patiently for my Nina and Big Dog to stop howling.

Yikes! Imagine if I had been making that kind of racket. And they were afraid that *I* was going to cause a problem.

Hmmmm. I think there's some appropriate human expression for this... like they should look in the mirror rather than point paws at me. Or something like that.

Anyway, I had a great night with my Nina. We watched a movie. I stayed as quiet as a kitten.

Early in the morning, before breakfast, Big Dog sneaked me back outside. He said that I couldn't sleep in any longer, or the maids might find me.

No problem. I've got this secret agent stuff down to a science now. I just tip-toed back to the elevator and away I went. I love adventures, especially with my humans.

Hey! I wonder if I can get frequent traveler miles for that trip. Nahhhh, probably not. That would just encourage me to come again.

21
GOOD GARDENING

*There is only one smartest dog in the world,
and every boy has it.*

--Anonymous

Most folk probably have no idea how to really garden. I am the exception. No one had to tell me things like, "Water the flowers every day." I always try to make the rounds of the various flowerbeds and do the best I can.

No one had to explain to me the importance of turning or aerating the soil. I just dig like mad and really toss that soil around. Yup, it's true.

I also patrol my gardens regularly so no pests would dare interfere. This takes a lot of time and attention, but staying as busy as a bee makes me as happy as a clam. And it works equally well with flowers and vegetables.

I have some favorite shrubs and flowers. Oh, man! When I lie down on them, they are sooo soft and spongy. (They make a perfect place to stretch out and just chew on a biscuit or a bone, by the way!)

You should know that most flowers aren't all that tasty, so I let them be. They are a lot of fun to run through, however, and I know my humans really like how good the blossoms look in my long fur.

Vegetables need a little more thought. I don't care much for things like broccoli and cauliflower, so I get my humans to pick them. I can actually pick a small zucchini or two. And the low-hanging green beans are just waiting to become my favorite crunchy snack food.

My favorite of all favorite veggies are those sweet little cherry tomatoes. Sometimes my Cathy human picks them and tosses them to me to catch in my mouth. Other times that takes too long. It's much easier for me to eat them right off the vines. They hang in great clumps like grapes, so I can get a whole bunch in one chomp!

I can pick the big tomatoes, too. I guess I'm colorblind though, because they laugh when I eat big green ones.

22
LEAF CHASING 🐾

Dogs are our link to paradise.
They don't know evil or jealousy or discontent.
To sit with a dog on a hillside on a glorious afternoon is to be
back in Eden, where doing nothing was not boring
  – Milan Kundera, Czech Author, Critic (1929 -)

Autumn is a great season! I get to romp and play with all those falling leaves. So many leaves to chase; so little time. But there are no flies on me!

I love having so many little playmates dancing all around me. I pounce and ground a couple of them, but as soon as I turn to stomp on another one, those first leaves tease me by jumping right back up in the air and swirling around. We go on like this for hours until the leaves are all tired out and lie down to go to sleep. Then I roll around all over them, so I can take some of my favorites inside to my humans.

They <u>really</u> like that, I know. They immediately gather them from me. I think they've started a whole collection of my leaves, because they always put them in the same big bucket. Hah! Just proves I've got great taste!

After a leafy attack!

Other times I just sit on the steps or lounge on the lawn and watch the leaves dance around. I don't know who does their choreography, but sometimes it's VERY fancy... a really amazing dog and pony show. All of a sudden, they zoom one direction or another in a big swirl. They flit about in the sky for a bit and then come swooping and swirling around some more.

It's wild to watch. After a while, all the leaves seem to blow away. Sigh. We sure do have fun while they're here though.

23

DOGGIE RESORT

The reason a dog has so many friends is that he wags his tail instead of his tongue.

--Anonymous

Sometimes when I get in the car to go for a ride, my humans give me a surprise. They take me to a doggie resort. I'm not kidding. My favorite is called the Sendaishi Pet Resort for dogs and cats.

I don't get to see the cats; they have their own section of the resort just for the felines. I hear that's because there are some dogs that don't like kitties.

Anyway, I've got to tell you that the whole idea of a pet resort really scared me at first. I mean, picture this. It's my first time. We go inside, and my humans sign me up for all sorts of great things like play time, swimming, and nature walks. Usually I get the full spa treatment, too, with pedicure and a fluffy hair-do included! However, on my first visit, I suddenly realized that my humans weren't going to be staying <u>with</u> me! "Oh, no! Don't leave me here with all these humans I don't know," I cried.

Feeling just like a fish out of water, I followed my initial plea with my very best desperate dog act… attaching myself to my human's thigh, pulling them toward the door so I could escape back to the safety of my car.

I tried playing possum. I even rolled over and bared my belly. "I give. I give. Uncle! Uncle!" Nothing seemed to work.

I guess I was scared that my humans might forget me and not come back, and I really do like my humans a lot! But, guess what?!!? They always come back for me. And, when they take me to the Resort, my humans always bring along some of my favorite treats.

Plus all the girls there have become my buddies. As soon as I arrive they start calling out, "Hi, Miles! Hi, Miles!" They're all very nice there. Hah! It's fun to go places and be so popular. I'm a very lucky dog.

24
SIGNALS THAT I LIKE YOU

> *Dogs are the most amazing creatures;*
> *they give unconditional love.*
> *They are the role models for being alive.*
> --Gilda Radner, American Actress (1946-1989)

When I'm playing games, it's with a bone or a stick or a ball. I never play with first impressions. I know that we're not supposed to be judgmental, but I can't help it. As soon as I meet people, I instantly know if I like them.

I always try to be polite. You know, I don't jump up on them. Well, I weigh a lot... over 100 pounds... way over 100 pounds. So, I could accidentally knock them down with all my pure exuberance. (Yup, I have a LOT of that.)

I always come check new folks out. If you really catch my fancy, I'll share my toys with you. I'll grab one toy in my mouth and shake it all around just to show you how it's done. I might even give it to you next, so you can try it. I have manners; I know how to share.

Another thing I like to do to get your attention is to stand close to you. No, I mean REEEALLY close.

When I press my side into you, it means you're supposed to pat me. Perfect! And don't stop until I tell you. If you do, it's okay. I'll just give you a firm nudge to remind you that I'm not through yet. Sometimes I'll even hold your paw. It just means that I like you, and I hope you like me.

Now, if you are really special, I'll roll over and let you rub my belly. I know that always makes humans feel so much better, so I try to do this often.

Hey! I'm just doing my part to keep my humans... <u>all</u> my humans... happy! It doesn't seem to matter what ails a human. They say that I'm the Buddha of Dogs – just rub my belly for luck and good health! Hah! The world is my oyster.

25
CIRCUS DOG

*Most dog owners are, at length,
able to teach themselves to obey their dog.*

--Anonymous

I can't begin to tell you how puzzling it is that my humans seem to think I need a career in the circus. They're always trying to teach me tricks.

Now I've heard the expression that "you can't teach an old dog new tricks." I think that's why my humans are still working on <u>old</u> tricks; keeps it easier for all of us.

Let's be serious. There are simply some things you shouldn't even try... like herding cats or teaching a pig to sing.

This circus trick business is very funny with my humans. Once they even taught my little seven-pound Bandit buddy how to ride on my back as though I was a pony. Well, I guess to Bandit I might have looked like a pony.

There are some tricks I've learned that truly suit me. They're no big deal really.

For instance, I'll shake hands with you. Simple, right? I mean, even humans can do that. But I take it one step further. I can actually shake hands with either paw. Hah! Try and get a human to do <u>that</u>! My own humans are so impressed with that one that they give me a cookie when I do it.

Now, if you knew me you might say that I look a lot like a black bear. Of course, that means you've never really seen one of those circus escapees. They're gruff as they lumber and roll along.

I'm a bit pigeon-toed, but I prance and sashay. Bears have long, hideous claws; I keep my toenails groomed in a perfect manicure.

They make a strange, whining roar sound; I have a handsome bark. The list goes on and on.

One <u>big</u> difference is that I am a <u>gentle</u> giant. If a door is only partially open, I won't push it the rest of the way. I'll sit politely behind it and mention softly that I'd like it opened. A simple "ahr-rahr-rahr-rahr" usually does the trick. Sometimes I have to repeat it because when I speak like this I'm using my quiet, indoor voice. My humans don't always hear me the first time.

Anyway, the humans tried to teach me one silly circus trick that really put my gentle nature to the test. They'd seen a miniature schnauzer do it with his humans, John and Jackie Gehrisch.

My humans figured if <u>that</u> little guy could do it, then good ol' Miles surely could, too.

Bogie (one talented Gehrisch Schnauzer)

So, they put three plastic, red Solo cups upside down on the floor. Then they put one of my tiny cookie treats under one of the cups. Hah! I can find that... with or without Toby Keith singing the Red Solo Cups song!

But noooo. They then start mixing up the cups, as though this was a shell game. When they stop, I go to the cup I think is hiding the cookie and give it a little nudge with my nose. I just want them to tell me if I've chosen the right cup.

But noo-ooo-ooo. They won't even give me a hint. They just mix them up again and wait for my nudge.

I finally figured out that they wanted me to tip the cup over to expose the cookie. So, I nudged it a little more firmly with my nose. I've got to tell you that this game is very disappointing. Most of the time I pick the wrong cup. Nothing is there. But I'm as stubborn as a mule, so I always get it by the second or third cup I try!

My poor humans. They are very persistent and really want me to figure this out. Okay... I can do this. But I'm certainly done nudging these silly little plastic cups.

One technique that works is to just pick up the cup I select in my teeth and toss it aside. This is too foolishly time-consuming however, because the cookie is rarely under the first cup I select.

There was this one time when I accidentally stepped on one of the cups and it flattened out like a pancake. That was cool. The best part is that there was a cookie! Hey, I learn pretty fast. In no time I could find my cookie prize in two seconds flat.

My humans hide it neatly under one cup. I watch them mix up the cups to try and confuse me. They step back. I simply move in and go bong, bong, bong – neatly flattening all three cups with my paw AND eating the cookie prize, all within two seconds. Beat <u>that</u> record! And my humans thought I might be a little slow. Hah! I'm actually really good at this trick stuff!

PS—I hate to let the cat out of the bag, so to speak, but it turns out this is just a stupid <u>human</u> trick. The fix was in all the while. The John and Jackie humans' dogs Mulligan and Bogie and Birdie couldn't have found the cookie on the first try either, except that their humans had a trick. They always left it in the middle spot after mixing the cups around and around. Hah! They got me! (Oh, well. I still get my cookie.)

26
NERVOUS AS A CAT

The greatest pleasure of a dog is that
you may make a fool of yourself with him,
and not only will he not scold you,
but he will make a fool of himself, too.
                --Samuel Butler, British Author (1835-1902)

It's true what they say – I've said it before, and I'll say it again: "I'm the cowardly lion of dogs." (Remember all my thunderstorm issues?) Where's that Wizard of Oz when I need him? If I only had some c-c-c-courage!

Actually, if I'm protecting my humans, I'm usually pretty cool. But if it's just me... well, okay. That's a very different story. If I hear strange sounds, I leap up and run to Big Dog's side.

Take what happened the other day. I was innocently scampering into my apartment under the porch. Suddenly, I stopped in my tracks. There was a ghost. Honestly. I didn't stick around to actually <u>see</u> it; hearing it was quite enough for me! It very clearly said, "Booo!"

See, I'm pretty smart, so I **know** that's ghost lingo. I ran for my life!!! Lickety split. But I couldn't find Big Dog anywhere. Help! Save me!

He was laughing when I finally found him. Hah! It had been Big Dog who was waiting in my pad, *pretending* to be a ghost. What a wise guy.

So, I flopped myself right down on the driveway so he could rub my belly. Then he laid down beside me. Seriously, right on the pavement! I held his paw until he calmed down. (Oh, I mean until I calmed down.)

Sheeeez, what an afternoon! He's such a kidder. He does this stuff to my Cathy human all the time – lurking behind doors or around a corner. Then he jumps out to scare her. She squeals. I come running. It's our routine. You think I'd get used to it, but it still gets me every time.

Now we've turned it into a sort of game. I'll hear him sneaking up on me, and he kinda jumps at me. Sometimes he even does this on his hands and knees so he's more my size. Well, I now kinda jump back at him. He laughs, and we do it again. I like making my Big Dog laugh! He'll get me over my nervousness yet.

27

DID YOU SAY "RIDE?"

*Did you ever notice
when you blow in a dog's face he gets mad at you?
But when you take him in the car
he sticks his head out the window.*
        --Stephen Bluestone, American Poet (1939 -)

When I hear the word "ride," I get so excited I can hardly contain my furry little self. Ride. Ride? YES!!!! Sometimes I get mixed up, like when my humans say something that rhymes with "ride." Sorry, but just try and say "snide," "outside," "beside," or "tried." All I hear is "ride," and, Baby, I am ready! If the doors are open, I'll be in the car in two shakes of a lamb's tail.

Yup, I'm right there… in the car and ready to roll. Sometimes I look so cute, they just have to let me come along anyway, even if it wasn't the original plan. (Miles' Lesson Learned: Being irresistible has its advantages.)

When I'm in the kitchen and the Cathy human opens <u>my</u> cupboard door, I know there's usually a treat coming. I grin like a Cheshire cat. I'm so happy I could just "purrrrr."
But bow-wow-WOW! Sometimes she brings out my leash, so I really jump for joy. I **<u>know</u>** that means "road trip." RIDE!!!

Yahooo! Then I really have to take charge to help my humans get organized and out of the house – fast! I mean, I am ready; let's go!

Once I'm in the car, I don't just ride. I look at everything. I love it! Sure, I like the breezes, but I really just like being there. And I help out so they know I'm appreciative. For example, I always make sure that I wash all the windows I touch. Hey, I'm just doing my part.

Oh, did I tell you that one of my cars is a Jaguar convertible? I mean, I've always liked cats, but this is really one very cool kitty. Big Dog literally chauffeurs me. I don't have to worry about opening a window to catch the breeze either. The whole top just drops into the back, and the windows go away too. It's all just one big awesome breeze!

My driver, Big Dog, helping me out of the car

I can't say that I know why *all* dogs seem to like to ride so much. There are so many great reasons that I love it. You know, lots of neat things to see, that wonderful wind, the vibration of the motor. Mostly, it's just another place to be with my humans!

Now… you tell me, just <u>what</u> could be better than that!?! I really do have the greatest life.

28
BOATING BOWZER

To his dog, every man is Napoleon;
hence the constant popularity of dogs.
    --Aldous Huxley, English Novelist (1894-1963)

I'm told that in my Newfy ancestry were some great fishermen. Well, they weren't really on the ships to catch the fish. They were there to help pull heavy nets and rescue the fishermen who fell overboard. Yup, the heroic tales of rescue are many.

Sometimes they had to swim several miles to land, pulling the humans the whole way. It sure must have helped to have these extra layers of fur for those outings. I hear the waters are very cold in the North Atlantic Ocean.

Anyway, my Big Dog loves boating. When I became big enough, my humans brought me to their boat.

Okay! This is cool. I love going anywhere with my humans. But I'd never before felt the ground rocking underneath me.

Visiting Maine, where we got our boat

Boating is a strange sensation. One minute I'm on terra firma, and the next minute, I'm floating. This is one weird kettle of fish.

The first night I spent on board we were in this great harbor on the coast of Maine. There were lots of other boats to see. But it was kind of eerie, too. I kept hearing ghost-like sounds. Creaking and oohing. It took me quite a while to figure out that there were no ghosts. The boats were just rubbing against these big bumper things along the docks as the water moved. It sounded kinda neat... once I stopped looking for the ghosts, that is.

It is strange on board a boat. The main level is sorta cool with my Big Dog Captain's cockpit and some nice soft cushioned benches. But getting into the cabin below is nothing less than a bizarre exercise in "let's torture the dog." The stairs are very open... like a ladder laid on a slant.

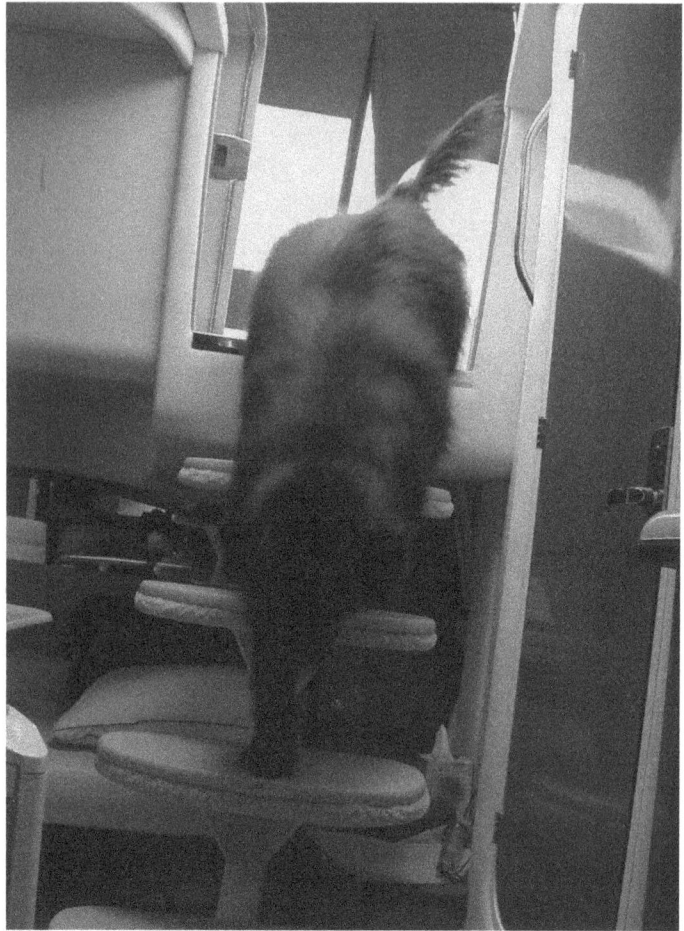
Gangway! Here I come!

I figured it out, but you better not be standing at the bottom when I go below. I'd bowl you over by accident, because I need a little runway space at the bottom to slow down!

Anyway, the cabin is neat, but it really had me goin' at first. I mean, there were my humans sitting on this big, raised platform watching TV. But when I looked the other way, I could see two more humans that looked just like MY humans. And woahhh! They had a big black dog. Hey, Pal, I'm not sharing my humans with any other dog. Back off, Buddy.

I barked at this strange dog, but he wouldn't leave. In fact, he just backed right back at me at the same time. When my humans came to pat me and tell me everything was okay, their twin humans did the same to this other dog!!

Awwww. How was I supposed to know it was just another stupid human trick done with a mirror? Hmmm... No wonder that other dog was both handsome and fearless. He was me! Kinda cool.

In the cabin of the boat

When it was time to go out on the water, I'll admit that I got very concerned. I swear there was a thunderstorm under the boat! Man, I just can't escape those things.

At first it was not bad at all – way off in the distance. But the faster Big Dog drove the boat, the closer the storm got. Didn't he know we were heading right for it?!?

Either that or the storm was catching up very fast. The closer and louder the storm got, the more concerned I was. We were all up on the top level of the boat, but I couldn't see any lightning. Still, it was getting louder and louder. I know that means closer and closer!

Suddenly, I couldn't take it any longer. I leapt onto my Cathy human's lap. Okay, so that wasn't going to work well because I'm bigger than she is. So, I immediately began my scramble to safety.

I pushed behind my Grandmother human, who was sitting beside my Cathy human. Then I squeezed between the boat wall and my Big Dog's Captain chair. Finally, I was safe. I was with Big Dog.

He'd save me from the raging storm. He actually let me sit on the other Captain chair right beside him.

First Mate Miles!

Wow! What a view – and the breeze is awesome from here. I now claim this chair for Miles. It's like sitting in a big open window and driving fast! Yahoooo!

Oh, yeah – Big Bad Noise. But this seat was so cool, it almost made me forget about the loud noise of that storm. My humans tried to assure me that there was no storm. They said it was just the noise of the boat's big engines getting louder as we traveled faster. I think they're teasing me.

Well, after a few more rides, I decided that they might be right. I'm still not big on loud noises, but boating sure is fun. I especially like patrolling the dock. My humans attach my leash to my collar and take me for a walk. Or perhaps I take them for a walk; it depends. This is <u>great</u>. I get to go the whole length of the dock and see all the other boats and say "hi" to lots of other dogs.

Ha-ha. It's fun to watch some of the humans on other boats scoop up their little miniature pooches when I approach. I figure they're afraid I might mistake their pups for morsels of cookies! Hah! They don't know that I'm much smarter than that!

Sometimes a bunch of the boats go anchor together somewhere on the water. Everybody swims and eats and stuff. It's fun. I really wish I had thumbs at these times.

See, the humans can climb up the ladders by themselves to get back into the boat from the water. I just can't hold the ladder. My humans have to help me back into the boat. Hah! Not easy – I guess I weigh even more when I'm soaking wet. Hah!

29
YOGA... MY WAY

The average dog is a nicer person than the average person.
-- Andrew Aitken "Andy" Rooney,
American Journalist & Commentator (1919 - 2011)

After a nice nap, it always seems like a good idea to lie around for a while. I mean, why get right up and start running around? It's not like I've got a schedule full of pressing appointments.

So, lounging is good. Stretching is also good. In fact, you should try this when you stand up: Reach your front paws wayyyy out in front of you, keeping them on the floor. Walk backwards but only step back with your back paws. Stretch, stretch, stretch! You can do it.

Here's a hint: I usually add a little singing – you know, really wide-mouthed with a big, high-pitched, yawn-like sound. Go ahead; try it. Goooood! I call this my Singing Downward Dog position.

Now return all four paws to the normal position on the floor. Breathe deeply.

Next we stretch our hind legs. Keep your back paws still on the floor and walk forward a bit using only your front paws. Notice that your back paws are now stretched out behind you. This feels so good on your back. Ooooh, yeah!

Another good stretched out singing note is good here, too. This is, of course, my Back Singing Downward Dog.

You can hold these positions as long as you like, by the way. It feels so good. The humans always smile when I exercise. I think they like the singing part best, because they join in with me when I sing. (Or yawn loudly, as in my particular case.)

Try getting one of your humans to scratch along the full length of your spine while you are in either of these fully stretched positions. If they'll keep doing that, believe me, you can hold these positions forever!!!

30
BONE APPETITE

A good dog deserves a good bone.

--Proverb

Typically, my humans keep my crunchy bowl nice and full. Then I can nibble whenever the urge strikes. I don't usually eat until they also sit down to dinner, but sometimes a chomp or two works to hold me over till suppertime... the very <u>best</u> time of day.

If my dish is empty, I can't dine. So, I must whine. Not a lot mind you. A simple, soft little "Roa-wahhh" usually gets a human's attention. A second whine, somewhat more annunciated like, "Arrooo-wahhhh" really gets them looking to see if I need one or both my dishes refilled.

It's easy. I've really got them trained. Humans are actually quite smart, you know. (The humans say they now can do this in a restaurant just as effectively. They call out something like, "Oh, waiter," but it still seems to work for them.) So, I know this whine and dine routine. I'm a pro.

They say I eat like a horse. I think that means that I'm not a particularly tidy eater, but I clean up the area around my dish when I'm through. Well, at least I clean up any of my crunchies that spill on the floor. My water dish is another matter entirely. After I drink, the humans always compliment me on how I've washed the floor... again.

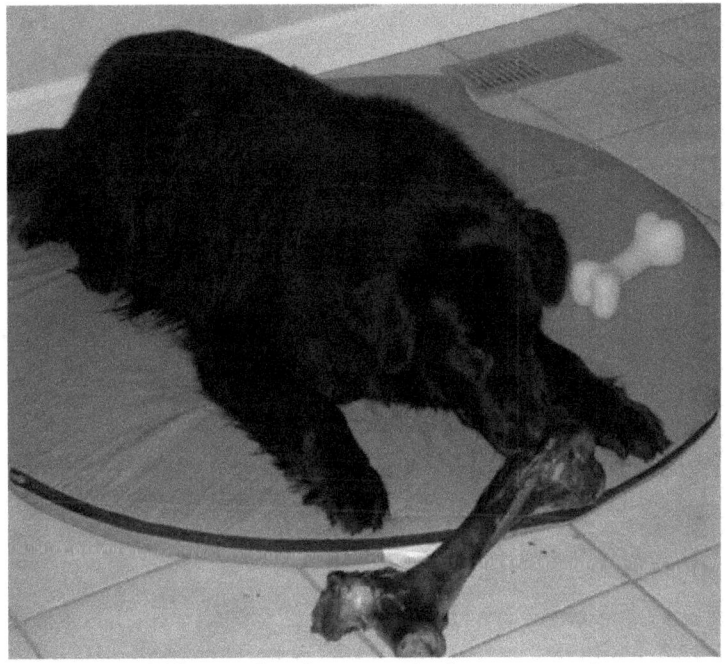

With one of my brontosaurus bones... yum!

They think I'm helping deliberately. I don't have the heart to tell them that it's just a coincidence. I mean, <u>you</u> try diving your face into a bowl of water to drink. To get it into your mouth you can't suck or use your tongue. You have to simply bite the water and gulp down whatever stays in your mouth.

It's a technique that works. You get to have a drink, wash your face and wash the floor all at the same time. Whoever said that dogs can't multi-task just wasn't paying attention.

31
CHEW TOYS

Never judge a dog's pedigree
by the kind of books he does not chew.
                              --Anonymous

As a dog, I simply gotta chew sometimes. Okay, most of the time. Usually I stick to my big ol' rawhide bone, but once in a while I just snap. Then I really end up in the doghouse.

There was the time my humans had given me this great new bed. It was awesome. Huge and so soft. I really liked it. But one night I got this strange urge to bite it. THAT felt great. I bit it again. One of my humans caught me and said, "No." Well, we dogs all know one basic truth. "No" means "not while my humans are watching." Duh!

Naturally, when they weren't looking I got back to quietly chewing. Soon I found big gobs of white fluffy stuffing that I could pull out. Wow, was this fun! I had stuffing all over the floor in no time.

My Cathy human was quite the spoil sport. She stuffed it all back inside the bed and sewed up my carefully gnawed hole. She very neatly turned the bed upside down, too... so that I wouldn't be encouraged to chew on or reopen my favorite spot.

Okay, I'm flexible. I found a new favorite spot. Yup! By morning I had every bit of stuffing pulled out of that bed... again. Too bad, because I really had liked it. But my humans said that this was not a game they were going to play with me, and they took that bed away from me. Oh, well... it was more fun than a barrel of monkeys for a minute there. I had fluff flying all over the kitchen.

After that first incident, I stuck to my rawhide bone... until this one day when one of Big Dog's buddies was visiting. Good ol' Norm. Now, he's a great guy, but something made me snap... again. I've got no other explanation.

I'd met his dog Joey once, probably a year earlier. He and I growled and barked at each other a lot; we never really hit it off, I guess. Still, it was unfair of me to take out my angst on poor Norm. I was a like a smarmy rat. I smelled Joey on Norm's jacket and just chewed the lining right out of one of his jacket sleeves. (I didn't tell anyone.)

When Norm got ready to leave and put his jacket on, he couldn't figure out why he couldn't get his arm into one sleeve. And, gee... why was it all wet?

Oops. Here we all were, but everyone looked straight at <u>me</u>. I guess that I looked guilty. I'll have to work on that.

Now, you'd certainly think that after this incident I'd have learned that this was the wrong way to greet our guests, right? Wrong again! Still, I didn't chew up any of our company's clothing again… for more than a year, that is.

Then one night… straight out of the blue… it happened. A whole bunch of company was here; we were all having a wonderful time. Suddenly, there was a giant hole in the sleeve of poor Alden's jacket.

I swear that I must have blacked out. I have no memory of actually doing the deed. But I did it all right; they caught me with the jacket still in my mouth. I just don't know how it got there. Seriously…one minute I was on the floor minding my own business. The next minute I was throwing myself on the mercy of the court. It's a good thing Alden is a buddy. (Of course, if I don't break this bad habit, our buddies won't want to come visit me anymore.)

Big Dog (aka The Ronald) with Alden & Lynda

Man, I don't know what comes over me sometimes. But you know what they say… a dog's gotta chew what a dog's gotta chew. (Yup. Another Miles' Rule.)

PS: Sorry, Norm! Sorry, Alden!

32
SNOW PATROL

The most affectionate creature in the world is a wet dog.
   -- Ambrose Bierce, American Journalist (1842-1914)

I absolutely love the season called Winter. Snowflakes feel soooo cool on my nose. I can sit in the middle of a snowstorm for hours. And I do.

Enjoying my snow cone weather

My humans laugh, saying that I look like a polar bear all covered with white snow. But it feels so gooood! Then when I come inside and get warmed up, it starts melting off me in big chunks. I guess I look like something the cat dragged in, but I'm all dry and fluffy again in no time.

After the snow collects on the ground, I also like to dive my face into it. *THAT* is the best!! I'll be trotting along and just poke my face into the snow and leave this long track. It's very refreshing. The snowflakes actually tingle as they melt on my nose. Oh, as I trot along, I also have learned to chomp and run, without ever breaking stride. I just keep poking my face into the snow to take a frosty bite. Step, two, three, bite, two, three, step, two, three, bite, two three. The winter world is my snow cone!

Sometimes the snow gets so deep I can't run through it any more. My Big Dog gets out his big snow-throwing machine and blows these great trails for me to run through. I especially like the ones that let me get closer to my birds and their feeders.

Big Dog clearing a trail to the bird feeders

My biggest challenge in deep snow comes in getting to the woods to do my very important personal business. The snow beside my trails is so much deeper than I am tall that it's tough. I leap as high as I can as I bound toward the woods. It's just a blur of white.

Sometimes I have to give up and do "my business" wherever I am when I get tired en route to the woods. Then I reverse and bound back through the snow to the door. Whew!

Off I go into the wild white yonder!

It's great exercise, especially if I ever decide to enter an Olympic high jump or hurdle event. My humans say that I look like a furry, black sea serpent when I do this. Hah!

Actually, my absolute favorite part of Winter is the never-ending supply of snack bars. I have easy cold storage for whatever bone or bones I'm in the process of devouring. I'm particularly fond of the ice-cold crispy edges the snow forms all along my walkways. I just hang out anywhere and chomp to my heart's delight.

The world is my snow cone!

As luck would have it, that's also the saddest part of Winter ending. My snack bars begin to diminish, and eventually they melt away altogether.

There's always one that lingers a big longer... all for me. At the end of the driveway beside the garage is this big mountain of snow that the snowplow driver collects for me. Ah, the pleasure it provides, slowly disintegrating in the Spring. I can lie there on the sun-warmed pavement and merely lean over a bit to chomp on the ice. I love it.

In the end I try to lie directly on top of the last tidbit of ice. I do this to try and shade it from the sun, so it won't go away. But, alas. One morning the worst has happened. I run to my ice spot, and it's gone. Siiiigh.

Oh, well. It will return next winter. In the meantime my humans humor me with these ice cubes from the kitchen. They call them Cheap Cookies. I only know they taste great, especially on a hot Summer day. My humans like them too. They fill their glasses and my water dish with them during the summer months.

I'll always share my cookies with my humans; they don't even need to ask.

33
LENDING A PAW

A watchdog guards your house, usually by sleeping where a burglar would awaken the household by falling over him.
--Anonymous

As you may know, a Newfoundland or Newfy or Newf is in what they call the Working Class group of dog breeds. This means that I am no slouch around the house. I like to pull my own weight, which is rather substantial. Sometimes I just hang out; that's true. But we all need to rest now and then to recharge our batteries.

For anyone who thinks that we dogs just lie around, I've got one thing to say: "Horsefeathers!" I mean, I work hard. I'm always helping my humans. As I've told you, they need me to wash the floor, so I start them out right by gulping from my water bowl and providing all the water they could possibly need all over the floor. It helps them. They simply need to zip around following me with the mop. Hey, it's the least I can do to help them out.

Then there are other official chores to do... like refilling the bird feeders. I let my Cathy human or Big Dog actually carry the food from the garage to the feeders, but I am right there at their side. I mean, someone has to be ready to chase away any pesky squirrels that might otherwise try to attack and steal those sunflower seeds. Then my poor birdies would starve.

Or how 'bout when it's time to take out the trash? The humans seem to work in shifts. Sometimes Big Dog does this, and sometimes my Cathy human does this, but EVERY week, Miles is right there going from the garage to the curb. And I'm talking two round trips since we have not one but two big trash cans. (Yeah, my humans create a lot of garbage!)

Now, I don't actually push the barrels. I let my humans do that. I trot alongside, biting at those pesky wheels. I'm not upset at the wheels; I'm not going to eat them. It's truly simple... the pure joy of chewing!

I also have a "clean up" responsibility that I take quite seriously. Suppose one of my humans is sitting eating dinner, and suddenly some delectable tidbit falls on the floor! Naturally, I'm watching, so I move right in and pick it up so they don't have to bend down or clean it up.

I can't pick it up in my paws – it's that "no thumbs" challenge again. But it all works out fine. I've learned that I can just pick it up in my mouth. Okay, I admit that I eat it, but we all know the ageless rule: "Whatever falls on the floor is Miles'."

This also applies to food being prepared in the kitchen. I try to encourage my Cathy human to allow me to be the food tester. I'm certainly not looking for free samples; I'm merely trying to ensure that my humans are eating good, safe food. I'm only thinking of them. (Wink, wink.)

Washing up after snacking

Anyway, my Cathy human hasn't yet caught on to this perfect job for me. When she's cooking, I plop down right at her feet, so she can't miss me. Now and then I even give her a little "Roooah" – just in case she hasn't noticed me yet. She always snickers and says the same thing, "Hope lives eternal in the heart of Miles." Hmmph!

Whatever that means! What I want to hear is, "Here's a little taste for you, Miles." But, nooo. She's got this "thing" about not giving me samples from either the preparation counters or the table while they dine. Sheeez. (Well, that's okay. When they sit down to eat, my dish is nearby, so I use that as my Suppertime, too.)

Anyway, back to my chores. One important role for all Newfies is watchdog. Wow, can I make everyone jump when I let out one of my giant barks! Well, I like to give them an early warning whenever someone has come into the driveway. Humans don't have great hearing, so they need me to do this.

Plus, I have to bark very loudly so that whoever is outside knows full well that I am right here... and I ain't no wimp. I go straight to the door to keep the new visitor on notice... until one of my humans says it's okay. NO one gets past the Miles-Mannered Man without their "say so." Not nobody; not no how.

Most of my other duties are supervisory in nature. I've always believed it's better to work smart than work hard! And someone has to monitor everything, so I am the watcher. Wherever the humans go, I watch.

Inspecting the spring flowers

We do laundry, dishes, water the plants, empty wastebaskets, set the table, clear the table, do the laundry, work in the office, and feed the dog. (Oh, that's me! Hah!) The list goes on and on. I can hardly sit still.

Whenever they have special little projects, I keep my humans in line. You know, inspecting the work at each stage along the way. I've gotten pretty good at sizing up their work… from putting up new lighting to painting and hanging wallpaper.

There's one thing I <u>don't</u> participate in… ever. That's vacuuming. Man, I *hate* that machine. It's wayyyy too noisy. But for all the other chores, I'm right there either helping or supervising.

Finally, when a task is completed, I roll over and let the humans rub my belly. They like that. It always makes them feel better, and it lets me show them that they did a good job. Smart dog, huh!

So, another Miles' Lesson Learned: "Be working class, but be classy!"

34
MAJOR PROJECTS

Yesterday I was a dog. Today I am a dog.
Tomorrow I'll probably still be a dog.
Sigh!
There's so little hope for advancement.
                          --Snoopy (in Charles Schulz' play
                          "You're a Good Man, Charlie Brown")

I think I found my humans just in time. When they got this house of ours it was surrounded by sand. Truly. There wasn't a single shrub or flower. Actually, the ground was covered with snow, so they didn't know that there wasn't even grass until the snow melted that first Spring. Surprise! They really needed me to help them whip this place into shape.

One of our first ordeals was some landscaping. Big Dog insisted on digging most of the holes, but I tried to follow suit and help him out. I guess I wasn't putting my holes in just the right places, because he'd just follow me around and fill up my holes, without even planting a shrub or tree in any of them. Eventually, we had great gardens filled with wonderful flowers, shrubs, and trees.

Then came some long, low stonewalls to edge around some raised flowerbeds. Wow was this fun! As fast as my Cathy human would build a wall, some silly chipmunk would burrow in, with me right behind it! Okay, so I just wanted to make sure that she did it right. Sometimes you have to do a project a second or third time, right? You should see the great patio and walkway we built one Summer. Now this was a lot of work. Big Dog worked with tons of rocks. I truly do mean tons. Even my Grand Poppy Burnham got in on this act.

It was a full family affair. We planned and planned. Digging was really a big part at the beginning, so we got a bulldozer to help. (Hah! I could have done that part, except that I was busy being in charge.) There was a lot of running around in the heat of Summer, let me tell you! Yup, I had to drink a lot of water. Big Dog did too. (And we got LOTS of those icy Cheap Cookies.) But we got it done, and it is lovely.

(L) Big Dog and Grand Poppy Burnham chatting about my work
(R) Big Dog building our barn

Because I am so talented in my post as General Contractor, we decided to build a little barn in the backyard. Now this was a challenge. Remember my no thumbs issue?

Well, it means that I can't carry lumber and beams and flooring and siding at all. Oh, well. The head of Canine Union 007 probably wouldn't be very impressed if I did any of that stuff anyway. So, I watch and supervise and let the humans know if it looks like some-thing is not quite right. And it works. We end up with a great barn! Oh, boy... another place to play!

Now I face a truly major project. Somehow I've got to convince Big Dog to be as sweet and gentle as I am when it comes to felines. You see, I've decided that I need a new kitty cat. NOT one of those black ones with the white stripe, mind you. I need a sweet little purr-meister... you know a cuddly fur ball to please my Cathy human and to keep the mice away... the mice that are sure to come now that we have a barn. I'm ready for a management job and a staff to supervise.

A kitty would be perfect. She'd actually run the place, being all about independence and all that. But I know she'd let me *think* that I'm in charge. Perfect! (Or purrrr-fect!)

Just showing Big Dog how well I'd get along with a kitty!

I'll have to work on Big Dog about this. He seems to think that my Cathy human is all the Cat we need.

35
WORKING DOG

Being patted is what it's all about.
   --Roger Caras, American Activist (1928-2001)

Sometimes my humans need a little extra help at their office. They might tell you that there are days that I have separation anxiety or severe thunderstorms are predicted or that there's some other reason that I need to stay very close to them. Hah! Don't you believe it. There are simply times when my duties expand to include their office because they need me with them all day.

The office is cool. It's in a city, so I get to see lots of new things on my walks. For instance, there are birds they call pigeons. They're pretty but very chubby and chatty. I've invited them to visit me at my house, but they've never come. They are truly dedicated city types... they think the country is just for us unsophisticated bumpkins. Whatever.

Inside the office is very nice too. I meet cool people, like CJ... always smiling and laughing. (She has a great laugh.) She talks to me and pats me.

And there's Sarah, who is so sweet. She likes everyone... but especially me, I'm sure. Okay... she like all the doggies that visit. She has pretty red hair... I like that. I wonder how I'd look as a redhead, but my humans won't let me try it out.

It's fun when the mailman or other delivery people come to the office. Hah! It's upstairs, so they can't stay in their trucks! Yup... even Brown. (Actually, I like Brown at the office; she's a nice lady.) Working the city beat they probably don't get to see lots of dogs. They all react with wide eyes when they first meet me. That's got to be because they think I look so much like a bear. Hah! They are all really neat people.

Mostly at the office, I lie on the floor and guard the fax machine and the printer. It's a lot of work, because that's a very busy area in the office. Sometimes I take a nap, go for a walk, or get a beverage to refresh myself. Soon, it's time to go home and catch up on my various patrol duties there.

You see, it doesn't really matter if I'm at home or at the office... or anywhere else. I am always ready to serve. With Big Dog's #1 youngest son, Adam, playing soccer at Merrimack College, I stepped right up to the plate to serve as mascot for the Warriors.

My Nina recognizing my toughness as the mascot

My Cathy human made me a great superhero cape and a Warrior headdress. I could wear it around the house as well as to the games.

Let me tell you how much the chicks dig superheroes. On my very first visit to the campus I found myself instantly surrounded by coeds. I mean, not just *any* coeds... I was being fawned over by SENIOR girls. Wow!

I had to point that out to young Adam. He was a Freshman, so he was pretty impressed. With just five minutes on campus, I had him beat. Wow!

One of the guys from their basketball team met me and wanted to know if I'd come be their mascot, too. I had to beg out of that duty, however. My feet just slip too much on gymnasium floor.

Merrimack College Mascot Miles on duty

Anyway, I think my services helped the soccer team. They were the underdogs... heh,heh... I love that expression. But they made it all the way to the New England Championship!!! That's so cool.

Miles' Lesson Learned: "A good dog's work is never done."

36
THE MUSICAL ME

A dog can express more with his tail in minutes than his owner can express with his tongue in hours.
                                        --Anonymous

I'm not much of a singer. (I told you earlier, I sort of just ya-a-a-awn... though with a sliding tone.) I'm more the Rex Harrison talk-song type. I can jibber jabber and rowah-grumpf with the best of them.

Some of the smaller pups I know are more the crooner types. They'll sing along with their humans – howl all night if you want. I just don't have that smooth tenor voice.

Still, I love music. Actually, I'm a dancing machine. I hardly ever just walk anywhere – I sashay. Truly. My humans say I really swing.

"Swing and sway with Sammy Kaye." That's what they say when they follow me down the road. I think it means that I've got style! And I do.

When I seriously want to put on the dog, I remind myself that I was named after jazz great Miles Davis. See! Music is part of who I am. Seriously, I'm quite a real rock 'n roller. If they crank up the tunes, I'm ready to hit the floor. I like it best when a human dances with me.

Big Dog doesn't like me to dance. He thinks it will encourage me to jump up on people, which could kinda scare folks who don't know me. Aw, it's no big woof. I suppose I could knock someone down, especially if they weren't in step with me.

Still, I love music, even if I'm just listening. I've grown exceptionally fond of Frank Sinatra. He's my Big Dog's all-time favorite. I think that I now know all the lyrics to all his songs from all 200+ of his albums. On the weekends, it's always time for Sunday with Sinatra at my house. We tune into the "Siriusly Sinatra" channel on the Sirius XM satellite radio. Croon away, Baby!

Oh, and Big Dog even put outdoor speakers in the backyard just for me. Now that's really the cat's pajamas.

37
WINTER OLYMPICS

*May I always be the kind of person
that my dog thinks I am.*

--Anonymous

You can probably imagine how excited I get when I'm romping with my humans. Sometimes, I guess I'm a bit too rambunctious. Okay... I'm like a bull in a china shop.

There was this one evening late last winter when all the snow that melted in the sun during the day had suddenly frozen invisibly after dark.

The humans called it Black Ice. So, here we are, doing a usual routine... taking out the trash barrels... but on ice.

First I scampered quick as a bunny after my Big Dog, who had the first barrel almost to the end of the driveway. Man, the pavement was sooo slippery it was hard for me to get going. My Cathy human called out to Big Dog to look out for me, because I was gaining on him fast, and she feared I couldn't stop.

Yikes! She was right! Thank goodness he stepped aside. Whew! I zoomed right past him. It was actually hysterical. I wasn't even moving my feet! I'd stopped running all right, but I kept zipping along. Cool.

My Cathy human was a little slow bringing the second barrel, so Big Dog had gone back and gotten it. She just doesn't move that well on ice, I guess. Aw – she felt so bad! So, I galloped back to make her feel better. Now you should know that I tried to stop; I really did. My feet stopped running, but my body just kept on moving! My Cathy human tried to side step cleverly, but my big ol' body did a little curve, and I clocked her.

Yup, I smacked into her low on her legs and at full speed. She flew right straight over me and landed face first on the ice. Oops! (Hey sports fans, I'll bet the slow motion instant replay was awesome though.)

Big Dog was very impressed. He says it was just like a bowling ball hitting the ten-pin. But I felt bad for my Cathy human. I almost broke her leg; this huge bruise and swelling stayed on her shin for a couple of months. Yikes! Here I try to protect her, and I'm the one who knocked her down.

Well, I gave her some extra nuzzles with my nose so she'd know I was sorry. I know she forgives me because she hugged me and gave me a cookie.

My humans have suggested that I should find a different winter sport other than Bowling for Humans. Figures! And I'm so naturally good at it. (Just teasing.)

38
THE GREAT CARJACKING CAPER

Number one way life would be different if dogs ran the world:
All motorists must drive with head out window.
 --David Letterman, American Television Host (1947 -)
From a famed "Top Ten" list on his late night television show

I didn't start out the day planning the crime. It just happened. Honest! It was this mild and gloriously sunny day, so my humans let me stay outdoors when they went to work. I love that. I finish my patrols and then flomp down into one of my favorite places to watch the world go by, protect the property, and await my human's return.

So, there I was, sitting in front of my house, minding my own business. Out of absolutely nowhere, the wind suddenly and ferociously attacked me. It sounded like a freight train.

Nobody told me we were supposed to get this huge wind storm. But it happened. I saw tree branches flying off the trees and lots of brush blowing around. That was very dramatic, but not bad.

Then it got much worse... louder, if that's possible. Chunks of big shingles started raining down on me as the wind began ripping up our roof. Yikes! Forget the Chicken Little theory of "the sky is falling." My house was literally attacking me. I couldn't run into my apartment under the porch if the house was falling, but I needed help... and fast!

I raced out of the yard, though I know it's against the rules. These were desperate times and called for desperate actions. No humans were in sight anywhere. I ran down the street. I still couldn't see anyone in sight. Help! Help! Help!

Couldn't anyone hear me? I guess not with that crazy wind howling so loudly and ripping the trees apart.

Just when I frantically thought I'd find no place to hide, I saw it. A shiny Corvette sports car was driving up the road. I boldly, though not at all calmly, stepped out and blocked his path. Okay, I admit it. I was actually jumping around like mad so the driver would know how urgent it was that he stop.

He did. I told the driver how scared I was. He was a good guy. He got out of his car and opened the passenger door for me. All right! I'm in! And safe!

Okay, okay... I know this was a dangerous move. I mean, this driver could have been a dog-napper. Boy, was I a lucky dog. This guy checked my tags and tracked down my Big Dog.

Whew! That was close. When Big Dog pulled up a few minutes later, I calmly stepped out of the sports car, barked my thank-you to the driver, and hopped into my own truck. This sure doesn't look like Kansas, Toto.

By the time Big Dog got me back home, my Cathy human was already cleaning up the mess of branches and shingles. Wow! The storm had ended, but the yard sure in shambles. The wind had flipped over a big metal table and broken our front door. I think I got out just in time.

For the next 24 hours I smartly stayed glued to my humans. No, I really mean it. I wasn't letting them out of my sight!

You already know that I am not a big fan of thunder and lightning. Well, I'm also just not into that "mean wind thing."

Note to self: Cancel plans to go parasailing.

39
ATTITUDE ADJUSTMENT

*Women and cats will do as they please,
and men and dogs should relax
and get used to the idea.*
--Robert A. Heinlein, American Writer (1907-1988)

They tell me that I have a great attitude. Well, why not? I live a fabulous life! My days are pretty well filled with eating, sleeping, playing, and chasing rabbits. (Hah! Just an expression, Bugsy!) So, I figure part of my job is to help others to smile a little more each day.

Humans can have a really bad day sometimes. They can be as cranky as a peach-orchard boar. But if they take one look at my smiling face, those humans just HAVE to smile back.

I've heard the humans say that you should smile at everyone you meet today because it makes them wonder what you've been up to. So, I smile at my humans when they come home after work, and sure enough. They always say, "Hey, Miles! What have you been up to today?" Wow! It really works.

Another important thing is to keep a cool head when all around you are losing theirs. So, if Big Dog is upset about something, I smile at him a little extra, and I try to give him a special nuzzle so he knows that I care. I even let him rub my belly. I talk to him softly and with lots of expression.

Sometimes I also put my paw on his paw or lay my head on his lap. Then he knowwwws that I'm with him all the way.

Yup, it works. He melts and tells me what a wonderful dog I am. Awwww, geee. It's great! He can be all kinds of cranky one minute, but I get him laughing in no time! Heck, I can get him laughing by doing something like sitting silly-style on the steps. (I do that a lot.)

Actually, it's very comfortable sitting Silly Style

Or I nuzzle my face into him until he just has to laugh because I am so cute. Hah! Imagine him calling someone as big as I am "cute!"

I also try to show my great pleasure by stretching and cooing. He actually giggles and tells me how wonderful I am, again and again. He also tells me how much he loves me. (But I know that.)

40
THE FUTURE

*No matter how little money
and how few possessions you own,
having a dog makes you rich.*
-- Louis Sabin, American Author

Just me, looking gorgeous

Every dog has its day, and if we play our cards right, it's a dog day every day! (Another Miles-erism for you.) Though we can never be sure what adventures lie ahead, we should have confidence that they'll be great. That's how I face life.

There will be more doggie buddies and more humans for me to claim and let rub my belly. I will continue to bound gleefully to greet them every time they come back home, even if they were just away for five minutes.

There will be more cars for me to ride in and more bones to bury. There will always be critters and birds for me to chase, snow chunks to chomp on, and brooks to play in.

Between naps, there will be more chores plus my vigilant guard duty. I'll have crunchies to consume, holes to dig, tricks to perform, and freshly mowed grasses to roll on.

So much to do and so little time! It's a good life. It's a dog's life. (Now I know what the humans mean when they say that!)

I love my humans, and I'm glad they love me. I look forward to every single day and night with them. I miss them terribly whenever they are away from me. For now though, this has been a lot of storytelling. It's time for a little refreshment and probably a nap.

I don't know about you, but both of those things are always good. Till next time, here are just a few of my tips for living well... just like the Miles-Mannered Man:

- Remember to love your humans thirty hours a day, eight days a week, and don't mess up the house too badly.

- Try not to shed or carry in too much dirt from outside.
- Play, play, and then play some more.
- Roll around on the grass, especially when it's freshly mowed.
- Romp gleefully in the fallen Autumn leaves and fresh Winter snows. (It's fun, and neither last.)
- When you dig, dig deeply, especially in places the humans have not yet found.
- Get skillful at a couple of simple tricks, so your humans will think you are even snazzier than the cat's meow.
- Take lots of naps, keep the snoring to a dull roar, and practice your yoga stretches when you rise.
- Soak up the sun on lovely days and find a cool shady haven when it's too hot.
- Show a little horse sense and stay out of the rain and snow, at least sometimes.
- Listen to your humans (especially when it might get you a cookie or a spot by the fireplace or their chair) and don't jump up on people.
- If your humans get upset with you, be the peacemaker and apologize; don't ever let them go to bed angry or annoyed.
- There's never a need to ration doggie kisses... and I mean never.
- Learn to use your indoor voice when inside the house, and, if there's any chance they might not let you sleep right beside them, lie very quietly so they might not see you. (And if they do see you, they'll think you're just too cute to disturb.)
- When humans are upset, quietly nuzzle them with your nose and look deep into their eyes so they'll know you care.

- Let all the best humans pat your head and rub your belly; only let them stop when <u>you've</u> had enough, and always show plenty of appreciation, so they'll want to do it again!
- Make sure that Brown (UPS) always knows who's the boss.
- And don't accept cookies and treats from strangers.

Whether you're a Poodle or a German Shepherd, a Maltipoo or a Mutt, a Collie or a Newfy, a Retriever or a Husky, a Pekinese or a Pit Bull, it just doesn't' matter. We're all in this life together. And it's a great life!

41
PAWS TO REMEMBER

If there are no dogs in Heaven,
then when I die I want to go where they went.
   --Will Rogers, American Humorist (1879 – 1935)

I know that dogs don't usually live as long as humans. That's why we have to love our humans so very much while we're here. We have less time on Earth to show you how important you are to us.

They (whoever "they" are) say that this is one of the big differences between dogs and humans. Humans act as though they'll live forever, taking loved ones for granted sometimes. We dogs live knowing, full well, that every single day is a miracle.

We miss our humans when you're gone for even one minute! After we're gone to Doggie Heaven, I believe that our humans miss us the most.

I once heard a poem, written by our John Gehrisch human friend. (Yeahhh, the same one who tried to get my humans to teach me that stupid cookie-under-the-Solo-cups bit.)

But he really loved another dog of his that was named Bandit. After his Bandit went to Doggie Heaven, John wrote a poem about the buddy he missed so dearly. I'm glad he's letting me share it with you here. (And I'm glad that he loved his Bandit so very much even *before* Bandit went to Heaven.)

WERE YOU ONLY A DOG?

I picked you out at the store named for pets.
All you wanted to do was play and kiss, if I let.
It was obvious, though, you'd only started to live.
A lot of love for all, you were ready to give.

When I paid no attention, and you I ignored,
Everything in the shop needed be explored.
It became clear right from the start
This was a puppy that would be very smart.

You were so tiny when I took you home.
Throughout the house you wanted to roam.
We gave you a baby blanket to have and play.
You carried it with you throughout the whole day.

Together the blanket we would pull and tug;
Your teeth were gritting, as I held you above the rug.
Any sock left on the floor you'd hide under the bed.
"Your name should be Bandit," is what we said.

We became best friends; I'd laugh till I'd cry
As you frantically tried to catch a live fly.
Remember at Christmas, you'd open your own present?
And when we said, "Bath," you'd disappear like a pheasant?
Remember on the bed, we we'd play cat and mouse?
How we'd play Hide and Seek all through the house?
All the tricks you would do: sit up, shake either hand,
Dance on your hind legs, like there was music and a band.

DOG DAYS IN THE LIFE OF THE MILES-MANNERED MAN

When I asked if you love me, you'd give a small growl…
"How could I ever doubt you," your face said with a scowl.
How you tried to console me, the time that I fell…
The secrets I told you, knowing you'd never tell.

Remember how you'd always follow, from room to room.
How you'd bite and attack the electric broom?
Hair blowing back as you co-captain the boat or help navigate the car…
Co-pilot the plane on both short trips and afar.

I'd ask, "Where's your leash?" when we were ready to go.
You'd run for it, carry it, and you'd never be slow.
The day you got lost, accidentally wandered away,
How excited you were, when a reward returned you my way.

Each time I left, atop the stairs you would be…
A shake, both hands, and a good-bye hug for me.
You would wait for me to disappear out the door;
Then throughout the house, you'd stand guard and explore.

If we were gone longer than you thought was right,
Paper in the wastebasket you'd pull out and bite.
Then when we'd come home, you'd lay in our laps.
We'd snuggle and play until time for taps.

You never, ever liked to go out in the rain,
But one day I awoke; it was different. It was pain.
Soon after, I lost you. Our time went so fast.
Oh, how I long for our times in the past.

Everyone you met, <u>you</u> they wanted to keep.
Now God has pulled rank on us all and put you to sleep.
No more will you finish the cone from the ice cream we eat,
Nor will spaghetti turn your mustache as red as a beet.

Your dog tags no longer jingle, as when you'd walk down the hall.
You no longer play fetch or catch with the ball.
There can be no more photos, in which you can pose…
No more smudges on windows from your little nose.

Now I miss those days, when it was I you would greet.
Atop the stairs there is no one for me to meet…
No tail wagging, ears back, type of smiles;
No papers from the wastebaskets in neat little piles.

My house, my life, my heart feel so empty this way,
But I know you're in Heaven; we'll be together again someday.
We all thought you a person; were we all in a fog?
After all, my little friend, were you "only" a dog?

IN LOVING MEMORY OF BANDIT
By John A. Gehrisch

Extra Treat #1
PRESIDENTIAL POOCHES

Children and dogs are as necessary to the welfare of the country as Wall Street and the railroads.
                                        --Harry S. Truman

If a dog will not come to you after having looked you in the face, you should go home and examine your conscience.
                                        --Woodrow Wilson

I was amazed to learn how many US Presidents have had dogs in the White House... as well as a rather wild assortment of other critters. And... just because I'm particularly fond of myself... I must point out that a few Presidents even had Newfoundlands! It's true! Ulysses S. Grant, Rutherford B. Hayes, and James Buchanan. You'll see the names of their Newfs on the following chart. Hmmmm... I just noticed something. It seems the "all caps" key got stuck every time the word "Newfoundland" got typed in the list. I wonder how that happened?

Some of the non-canine critters are fascinating. Naturally there have been lots of kitty cats in the White House over the years, but in addition to cats and dogs, check this out:

Rabbit	Jimmy Carter 1977-1981
Fish	Richard Nixon 1969-1974
Canary (Robin), parakeets (Bluebell &	John F. Kennedy

Marybelle), ponies (Macaroni, Tex, and Leprechaun), horse (Sardar), hamsters (Debbie & Billie), rabbit (Zsa Zsa)	1961-1963
Pig, squirrel	Dwight D. Eisenhower 1953-1961
Opossum	Herbert Hoover 1929-1933
White canary (Snowflake), canaries (Nip & Tuck), thrush (Old Bill), goose (Enoch), a bear, mockingbird, raccoons (Rebecca & Horace), donkey (Ebeneezer), bobcat (Smokey), lion cubs, wallaby, pigmy hippo, and an antelope	Calvin Coolidge 1923-1929
Canaries	Warren Harding 1921-1923
Tobacco-chewing ram (Old Ike), sheep and chickens	Woodrow Wilson 1913-1921
Cow (Pauline Wayne)	William Taft 1909-1913
Badger (Josiah), calico pony (Algonquin), macaw (Eli), piebald rat (Jonathan), two kangaroo rats, garter snake (Emily Spinach), lizard (Bill), 12 horses, bear (Jonathan Edwards), 5 guinea pigs (Admiral Dewey, Dr. Johnson, Bishop Doane, Fighting Bob Evans, and Father O'Grady), rabbit (Peter), pig (Maude), blue macaw (Eli Yale), one-legged rooster (Baron Spreckle), a barn owl, a flying squirrel, lion, hyena, wildcat, coyote, parrots, zebra, raccoon, and lots of horses	Theodore Roosevelt 1901-1909
Mexican double-yellow-headed parrot	William McKinley

	1897-1901
Billy goat (His Whiskers) and an opossum	Benjamin Harrison 1889-1893
Canaries and mockingbirds	Grover Cleveland 1885-1889
Mare (Kit) and fish	James Garfield 1881-1885
Pedigreed Jersey cows, the first Siamese kitten to reach America (Grim), goat, canaries, several horses, mockingbird	Rutherford Hayes 1877-1881
Horses (Jeff Davis, Julia, Jennie, Mary, Butcher Boy, Cincinnatus, Egypt, and St. Louis), ponies (Reb & Billy Button), pigs, parrot, roosters and gamecocks	Ulysses S. Grant 1869-1877
Family of mice	Andrew Johnson 1865-1869
Pig, ponies, white rabbit, goats (Nanny & Nanko) — They road with Lincoln in the Presidential carriage, and a turkey (Jack)	Abraham Lincoln 1861-1865
Herd of elephants from the King of Siam, pair of bald eagles	James Buchanan 1857-1861
Horse (Old Whitey) and canary	Zachary Taylor 1849-1850
Horse	James Polk 1845-1849
Horse (The General)	John Tyler 1841-1845
Billy goat and a New Durham cow	William Henry Harrison 1841
Pair of tiger cubs from the Sultan of Oman	Martin Van Buren 1837-1841
Horses (Truxton, Sam Patches, Emily, Lady Nashville, and Bolivia), ponies, and a parrot (Pol)	Andrew Jackson 1829-1837
Alligator from the Marquis de Lafayette	John Quincy Adams

and silkworms	1825-1829
Green parrot (Macaw) and sheep	James Madison 1809-1817
Mockingbird and a pair of bear cubs (gift from explorers Lewis and Clark)	Thomas Jefferson 1801-1809
Horses	John Adams 1797-1801
Horses (especially his personal favorite, Nelson) and a parrot (Polly)	George Washington 1789-1797

If you want a friend in Washington, get a dog.
--Harry S. Truman

Naturally, dogs have been the most popular Presidential pets. Very rarely do the history books find someone serving in the White House and not having any pets at all.

Dogs are particularly important to our Presidents. We canines are great at reducing stress... and I can only imagine how stressful the top job in the White House is. And there's no better listener than a good dog, so these pets in particular are certainly the first to have heard many a President developing an idea or deliberating some course of action. Best of all... we never talk; we are great at keeping secrets.

Here's a look at some of the dogs that have graced our nation as Presidential pets:

Portuguese Water Dog (Bo & Sunny)	Barack Obama 2009 - 2017
English Springer Spaniel (Spot "Spotty" Fletcher), Scottish Terrier (Barney), Scottish Terrier (Miss Beazley)	George W. Bush 2001-2009
Labrador Retriever (Buddy)	Bill Clinton 1993-2001

Springer Spaniel (Millie, who also wrote a book!)	George Bush 1989-1993
Bouvier des Fladres (Lucky), King Charles Cavalier Spaniel (Rex)	Ronald Reagan 1981-1989
Spaniel (Grits)	Jimmy Carter 1977-1981
Golden Retriever (Liberty)	Gerald Ford 1974-1977
Cocker Spaniel (Checkers), French Poodle (Vicky), Terrier (Pasha), and Irish Setter (King Timahoe)	Richard Nixon 1969-1974
Mongrels (Edgar & Yuki), White Collie (Blanco), 2 Beagles (Him and Her), Beagle (Freckles) — Him's pup	Lyndon Johnson (1963-1969)
Welsh Terrier (Charlie), German Shepherd (Clipper), a famous dog (Pushinka) — a gift to Caroline from Soviet Premier Nikita Khrushchev; Pushinka was daughter to the first dog in space, Strelka; they also had the puppies of Charlie and Pushinka (Blackie, Butterfly, Streaker and White Tips)	John F Kennedy 1961-1963
Weimaraner (Heidi)	Dwight D Eisenhower 1953-1961
Irish Setter (Mike) and Mongrel (Feller)	Harry S Truman 1945-1953
German Shepherd (Major), Scottish Terrier (Meggie), Llewellyn Setter (Winks), English Sheepdog (Tiny), Great Dane (President), Scottish Terrier (Fala) — memorialized in a statue beside one of his master in Washington, DC, and a Mastiff (Blaze)	Franklin D Roosevelt 1933-1945
German Shepherds (King Tut & Pat), Fox Terriers (Big Ben & Sonnie), Scotch	Herbert Hoover 1929-1933

Collie (Glen), Malamute (Yukon), Irish Wolfhound (Patrick), Setter (Eaglehurst Gillette), and an Elkhound (Weejie)	
Collies (Rob Roy, Ruby Rough, Bessie, Prudence Prim), Terrier (Peter Pan), Sheepdog (Calamity Jane), Airedale (Paul Pry), Chows (Tiny Tim & Blackberry), Bulldog (Boston Beans), German Shepherd (King Kole), bird dog (Palo Alto)	Calvin Coolidge 1923-1929
Airedale (Laddie Boy) and English Bulldog (Old Boy)	Warren Harding 1921-1923
Bull Terrier (Pete), Chesapeake Retriever (Sailor Boy), Terriers (Jack & Pete), Mongrel (Skip), Pekingese (Manchu) — gift to Alice from the last empress of China	Theodore Roosevelt 1901-1909
Favorite dog (Dash) and various others	Benjamin Harrison 1889-1893
Japanese Poodle	Grover Cleveland 1885-1889
Mongrel (Veto)	James Garfield 1881-1885
NEWFOUNDLAND (Dot), German Shepherds (Hector & Nellie), Greyhound (Duke), and an English Mastiff (Hector)	Rutherford B. Hayes 1877-1881
NEWFOUNDLAND (Faithful)	Ulysses S. Grant 1869-1877
Mongrel (Fido) and several other dogs	Abraham Lincoln 1861-1865
NEWFOUNDLAND (Lara)	James Buchanan 1857-1861
Greyhound (Le Beau) and a pair of Italian wolfhounds	John Tyler 1841-1845

Spaniel	James Monroe 1817-1825
A pair of Briards	Thomas Jefferson 1801-1809
A pair of dogs (Juno & Satan)	John Adams 1797-1801
36 Hounds	George Washington 1789-1797

Now, I won't list the handful of Presidents who didn't have ANY pets, never mind no <u>dog</u>! We'll just let it go for now under the assumption that, of course they had at least one pet, even if not a dog. Perhaps good records simply weren't maintained or it could have been a matter of national security. Yeah, maybe they were very allergic to animals or something.

Regardless, since the White House was built, historians say that more than 400 pets have made it their home. Only George Washington's pets didn't get to live in the White House, since it wasn't built until John Adam's administration.

Extra Treat #2

OTHER FAMOUS AND HEROIC DOGS

> *Histories are more full of examples*
> *of the fidelity of dogs than of friends.*
> --Alexander Pope,
> English Poet (1688-1744)

Some experts think that we Newfoundland dogs descended from the Tibetan Mastiff. Others think we were Leif Ericsson's Viking "bear dogs" and that he brought us to Newfoundland. History shows that in the 19th century we Newfys or Newfies or Newfs became a European status symbol. In fact, we became Great Britain's number one imported item! And we were even used to re-establish the Alpine rescue dogs after so many St. Bernards died in a distemper epidemic.

> *Newfoundland dogs are good to save children from drowning,*
> *but you must have a pond of water handy and a child,*
> *or else there will be no profit in boarding a Newfoundland.*
> --Josh Billings (Henry Wheeler Shaw),
> American Humorist (1818-1885)

In my Miles-Mannered viewpoint, THAT quote reflects a rather cynical viewpoint. There are hundreds of documented water rescues made by Newfs, and not just children. That made us very popular partners on fishing boats. We are really good swimmers because of our powerful strength, webbed feet, and resistance to the cold. There may not be as much call for water rescues these days, but you never know. So, we are always ready.

As dogs, our loyalty and devotion to our humans is unsurpassed. We never falter in the line of duty. In early years in the United States and Canada, the Newfoundland was used for hauling in nets on fishing boats, carrying boat lines to shore, recovering anything that fell overboard and for regularly rescuing shipwrecked and drowning victims. Newfs are also credited with hauling lumber, pulling mail sleds, delivering milk and carrying loads in packs.

Naturally, there are dog adventure and lifesaving heroes of many breeds. (Newfies are simply my favorite, since all the pictures look just like ME!) Hey, we've even got a Beanie Baby Newfoundland, named Seadog.

And in the 1800's, a life-sized cast iron Newfoundland statue was erected at what is now Belmont University in Nashville, Tennessee. In 1925, the Newfoundland dog was featured on the one-half cent US postage stamp… the FIRST dog to get his own stamp.

Of course, the British American Bank Note Company in Montreal beat the US by creating the world's first stamp featuring a dog. The Newfoundland dog series used for stocks and bonds started in 1887 and continued through 1898.

Later, in 1913, the Newfoundland appeared on a stamp in Canada again. This time it was for tobacco revenue stamps. Whew! Newfies were smokin'!

There have been lots of dogs of all types made famous in movies, television, and cartoons. Benji, Lassie, Rin Tin Tin, Toto, Deputy Dawg, Goofy, Odie, Scooby Doo, and Snoopy are among my personal favorites. I particularly liked the Newfoundland named "**Mother Theresa**" in the 2004 movie "Must Love Dogs."

"**Boatswain**" is a famous Newfoundland dog captured in Lord Byron's poem in 1808. Literary buffs probably already know that "**Nana**" in "Peter Pan" is also a Newfoundland dog. Ahhh! That's true. As Tinkerbelle said, "Believe."

But in real life are the real heroes, in a lot of varieties.

Chelsea, a Golden Retriever in Texas, saved her owner and a neighbor from two gunmen, by lunging at them. (Chelsea was shot in the shoulder and recovered fully.)

Brandy, an English Springer Spaniel puppy in Arizona was home with her mistress one night, while her master was at work. An intruder with a machine gun broke in and opened fire, hitting Brandy's mistress twice. Brandy growled, barked and bit the intruder, who emptied five bullets into the dog's chest and face before finally fleeing the house. That intruder was later found by authorities and shot in a gun battle. Oh, and by the way, after her mistress spent seventeen days in the hospital, and Brandy underwent lots of veterinary surgery, both recovered completely.

Lindsey, a Newfoundland in British Columbia, barked ferociously to awaken her owners when a man was attacking a neighbor with a hammer late one night. Lindsey's action enabled her owners to call the police and get the badly wounded woman into the safety of their home. Everyone properly credits Lindsey with saving her neighbor's life that night.

Barry, a Newfoundland, is credited with keeping his mistress alive following a severe car accident. In a two-hour wait for an ambulance in a 10-degree cold, he laid by her side without moving. Doctors said Barry's body warmth was the only reason she survived.

Dusty, a Bichon from Minnesota, was thrown from his owner's car when it rolled off a rain-soaked dirt road and landed in a forest. Dusty made his way back to the road, jumping up and down to get the attention of passing motorists. When a driver stopped and called for help, Dusty went back and stood guard over his owner until help arrived.

Tang, a Collie from Texas leaped in front of an oncoming vehicle and pushed some young children to the curb.

Duke, a Welsh Corgi in California, pulled his 85-year-old owner out of the way of a truck going the wrong way on the street where they were walking.

Top, a Great Dane, pushed his neighbor out of the path of an oncoming speeding truck in California.

Twang, a Collie in Chicago, pushed four children out of the path of a speeding automobile.

Bubba, a Black Labrador in Pennsylvania, rescued his 9-year-old master by pulling him out of a swift creek.

Patty, a Yellow Labrador Retriever from Maine, saved her owner from drowning during a winter sea, duck hunting trip. His boat had capsized in the frigid northern Atlantic Ocean. He knew he'd never make it to shore, but Patty let him hold her tail and she paddled them safely to land.

Boo, a 10-month-old Newfoundland puppy with no training, swam out into rough water to save a man from drowning.

Begger, a Saint Bernard, pulled his 3-year-old master from a river, saving him from drowning.

Chester, a Chesapeake Bay Retriever, rescued his 5-year-old master from a fast creek.

Mijo, a Saint Bernard, pulled a young girl from a muddy pit of water where she was drowning.

Moby, a Newfoundland in California, is one of the most important crew members on board Rapture Marine Expeditions. Up to 150 young people are on board at a time. Moby swims with them to detect any kids getting into trouble. The children are instructed to just grab onto Moby, and he pulls them through the swift currents back to the boat.

Blue, an Australian Blue Heeler from Florida, fought off an alligator and saved his elderly mistress when she had fallen behind her house.

Sundance, a Golden Retriever in upstate New York, rescued a 3-year-old girl from an escaped 8-foot python.

Jake, a Boxer in Arizona, saved his 7-year-old owner from a rattlesnake.

Leo, a Poodle in Texas, suffered numerous bites while protecting two children from a diamondback rattlesnake.

Weela, an American Pit Bull Terrier, suddenly pushed his 11-year-old master out of the way, just in time to save the boy. Weela took a rattlesnake fang bite right in the face, but she fortunately recovered.

Spike, an American Pitbull Terrier in Arizona, started barking loudly as his owner prepared to dive into his swimming pool. Sensing something must be wrong, his owner turned on the pool lights and found a five-foot Western Diamondback Rattlesnake coiled up on the water's surface, directly in his swimming path.

Sadie, a 45-pound English Setter in Tennessee, dragged her owner a third of a mile out of the woods after he suffered a serious heart attack while hunting.

Sparky, a 130-lb yellow Labrador Retriever, dragged his 227-lb master home when he'd collapsed from a heart attack on their morning walk.

Mimi, a miniature Poodle in Connecticut, alerted her entire family of eight that their house was on fire; they all escaped unharmed.

Ivan, a Lab/Husky mix from Washington woke his hearing-impaired owner from a sound sleep by jumping on his chest when a fire broke out in their apartment. Ivan then went to the daughter's room and pulled the 3-year-old out the front door to safety.

Budweiser, a St. Bernard, dragged two of his owner's grandchildren out of a burning house in South Carolina.

Villa, a Newfoundland in New Jersey, leaped a 5-foot fence to rescue an 11-year-old girl who'd been blown by 60 mph winds into a large snowdrift.

In a massive 2005 Los Angeles train collision, **Hero**, a disaster search dog, helped rescuers find every survivor in the twisted wreckage.

History is full of famous dogs, from explorers and warriors to devoted companions. Journals are filled with one amazing account after another. Some famous dogs were considered pets or companions. Others literally served alongside our military forces.

Rigel, a Newfoundland belonging to the first officer on the ill-fated Titantic, was the only dog to survive the tragedy. He actually swam in the icy waters for three hours and then guided the boatloads of survivors to the Carpathia, the first ship to reach the scene. The passengers in the fourth lifeboat were too weak to realize they'd drifted under the Carpathia's starboard bow. Rigel swam right in front of the troubled boat and barked loudly till he got the Captain's attention, saving all the people in the lifeboat.

Stubby, a stray mongrel, became a heroic military dog in 17 World War I battles. He regularly walked the front line boosting morale, gave early warnings of gas attacks, woke up a sleeping sentry to alert him to a German attack, ferreted out a German spy, and earned numerous medals. Stubby was made a lifetime member of the American Legion and marched in every parade for the rest of his life.

Henri was Napoleon's Newfoundland. He never left the "little general's" side.

Chips, a dog hero of the 3rd Military Police platoon in World War II, was actually promoted by General Eisenhower to Private First Class. He'd found a hidden German machine gun nest in Sicily, Italy and pounced on the German who was operating the weapon. Although he was wounded, Chips was solely responsible for the soldiers' abrupt surrender. (By the way, Walt Disney studios did a TV movie about him called, "Chips, the War Dog.")

Two Newfoundland dogs were used during World War II for hauling supplies and ammunition in blizzard conditions in Alaska and the Aleutian Islands,

Gander was the Newfoundland mascot of Quebec City's Royal Rifles of Canada. Officially he was called Regimental Mascot Sgt. Gander and is credited with saving the troops in at least three documented battles. His last heroic act was to take a Japanese grenade in his mouth and run away from the trapped group of soldiers. Gander's heroism was honored with Canada's highest medal.

Four thousand dogs were recruited and used to protect US troops in the Vietnam War. It's estimated that they prevented 10,000 US casualties.

Now I've even heard there is actually a National War Dogs Monument in Washington, DC to recognize the service and sacrifice of thousands of US War Dogs.

Oolam was the Newfoundland that traveled to North America with her master, Norse explorer, Leif Erickson. When the Vikings came from Europe around 1000 A.D. it is said that Oolam saved the lives of five Vikings who had fallen overboard.

American colonist Samuel Adams had a Newfoundland named **QueQue**. When the British blockaded the Boston Harbor, the Newf proved to be an early patriot and pulled many pranks on the Redcoats.

Seaman was Meriwether Lewis's Newfoundland and traveled with him during the Lewis and Clark Expedition; his great swimming, tracking, hunting and watch dog abilities proved very valuable. Plus, he intimidated the American Indians, who thought Seaman was a domesticated bear.

Tang was a Newfoundland that saved everyone on a steamship called Ethie in 1919. In a bad storm, following a shipwreck on rocks, the seas were too rough for lifeboats and the boat was breaking up. Tang took the line in his mouth and swam through the breakers and rocks to bring the line to shore. That line was used to bring everyone safely to shore, one by one.

Laika (nicknamed **Mutnik**) was the first dog in space when she was launched into orbit in Sputnik II in 1957 by the Russians. Sadly, she died during her journey from overheating and stress.

Belka (Squirrel in Russian) and **Strelka** (Little Arrow) orbited the Earth in 1960 in Sputnik 5 and returned safely to earth one day later.

Robot is the dog who discovered the Paleolithic cave paintings at Lascaux in France in 1940.

Bobo was a Newfoundland who spent his life in the early 1950s ringing doorbells for children and leading the children to the Cleary School for the Deaf every day. After his passing, another Newfoundland puppy, **Penguin**, was found to carry on the tradition.

Brumis was the Newfoundland that was the beloved companion of the late Robert Kennedy. He was permitted to sit in at top-secret meetings.

Balto and **Togo** were the lead dogs on sled-dog teams that delivered the diphtheria antitoxin from Anchorage to Nome, Alaska, during an epidemic in 1925.

--- --- --- --- --- --- --- --- ---

And we must _never_ forget the many, many brave search and rescue dogs that worked tirelessly, searching the rubble of the World Trade Center towers following the 9/11 attacks on America in 2001.

Getting back to my personal favorite breed... Lots of famous people have owned Newfies. Get a load of this partial list:

Troy Aikman, football quarterback
Burt Bacharach, composer
JM Barrie, author of "Peter Pan"
Carol Bayer Sager, actress
Humphrey Bogart, actor
Victor Borge, comedian and pianist
Dave Brubeck, jazz pianist
Bing Crosby, singer and actor
Charles Dickens, author
Emily Dickinson, poet
Boomer Esiason, football quarterback
Harrison Ford, actor
Ben Franklin, Colonial statesman & inventor
Jerry Garcia, of "The Grateful Dead"
Barry Goldwater, US Senator & Presidential candidate
Ulysses S. Grant, US President
Warren Harding, US President
Ernest Hemingway, author
Don Imus, radio personality & talk show host
Robert F. Kennedy, US Attorney General & US Senator
Mario Lemieux, hockey star
John Madden, NFL broadcaster
Nina Martin, life student & human extraordinaire
George McGovern, US Congressman & Presidential candidate
Willie Nelson, country singer
Eugene O'Neill, author
Paul Revere, Colonial patriot
Franklin D. Roosevelt, US President
Jay Severin, radio talk show host
Donald Sutherland, actor
Sally Struthers, actress
Shania Twain, country singer

Robert Wagner, actor
George Washington, US President
Paul Winter, composer & musician
Andrew and Jamie Wyeth, artists
Meriwether Lewis, explorer
Lord Byron, British poet & author
Sting, singer
Orville and Wilbur Wright, inventors of the airplane

Dogs… everyone's best friends!!!

Extra Treat #3

MILES' FAVORITE RECIPES

*If you pick up a starving dog and make him prosperous,
he will not bite you.
This is the principal difference between dog and man.*
         --Mark Twain (Samuel Langhorne Clemens),
              American Author & Humorist (1835-1910)

I'll start with my all-time absolute favorite recipe. It was created by my Cathy human's Dad, Bob Burnham. Because she calls him Poppy, that makes him my Grand Poppy. He says these are not just treats; he says they also make me even smarter! I just know they taste GREAT.

Grand Poppy's Brain Food
Chunk of fresh beef liver

Place the liver in a large pot of boiling water. Reduce the heat and simmer 10 minutes. Drain and rinse till cool. Cut liver in small, bite-sized pieces. Place a few (one day's portion) in several small snack-sized plastic bags and freeze all but one bag. Store the bag you are using in the refrigerator.

Tip:
You can save the water from cooking the liver, if you'd like... it is GREAT poured into ice cube trays and frozen as treats for us four-legged folks!

Bacon Biscuits

¾ c bacon grease (softened or still liquid)
5 c flour (white or mixed with whole wheat)
1 tsp salt
2 extra-large eggs
1 c milk
½ c beef broth (canned is fine)

Cream the flour & salt into the bacon grease in a medium bowl. Stir in the eggs; then add the milk and broth gradually. Roll into 1-2" balls and place 1" apart on a greased baking sheet. Bake at 350°F for 25 minutes. Cool on wire racks. Store at room temperature or freeze for longer storage.

Peanut Butter Cookies

¼ c peanut butter (creamy or chunky)
1 extra-large egg
¼ c vegetable oil
2 T honey
¾ c quick oatmeal
1½ c flour
1 tsp baking powder

Cream together the peanut butter, egg, oil, and honey. Mix in the oatmeal, flour and baking powder. (If the consistency needs a little more moisture, gradually add some water.) Form into 1" balls and place on ungreased baking sheet. Flatten to ¼" thickness with the tines of a fork, just as with peanut butter cookies for people. Bake at 325°F for 15 minutes. Makes 2 dozen cookies for the DOG. (Hey humans: No sneaking our treats!)

Cheesy Biscuits

1 c boiling water
1 c quick oats
1/3 c butter, at room temp
1 c shredded cheddar cheese
¾ c cornmeal
½ c milk

1 extra large egg, beaten
1 T freshly chopped parsley
2 T bouillon granules (chicken or beef)
2-½ c white or whole wheat flour

Stir together the water, oats and butter in a medium bowl and set aside for 10 minutes. Combine the cheese, cornmeal, milk, egg, parsley, and bouillon in a small bowl. Stir into the oats. Stir in the flour, ½ cup at a time, mixing well after each addition. The dough will be stiff. On a lightly floured surface, knead in additional flour until the dough no longer feels sticky. Roll to ½" thick and cut into cookie cutter shapes. Place 1" apart on greased baking sheet. Bake at 325°F for 30-35 minutes until golden. Cool on wire racks. Refrigerate biscuits; these also freeze very well.

Biscuits

2½ c flour (white or wheat)
½ c powdered dry milk
¼ c dried soup mix (any type your dog likes, but not onion)

6 T butter, softened
1 extra-large egg
½ c chilled beef broth

Mix together the flour, powdered milk, and soup mix in small bowl. In medium bowl, cream the butter with the egg. Stir in the broth. Stir in the dry ingredients and mix well. On floured surface, roll to ½" thick and cut into cookie cutter shapes. Place on greased baking sheet. Bake at 350°F for 20-25 minutes. Cool and store at room temperature in open container to keep crisp.

Note: You can replace soup mix with 3-4 T peanut butter. Just cream it into the butter before adding the egg.

Banana Chews

½ large, soft banana, mashed
1 extra-large egg, beaten
1 c quick oats
1/3 c milk
½ c flour
1/8 c minute rice

Mix ingredients together and spread on microwave-safe plate or baking dish. Microwave on high for 3 to 3-½ minutes. Let cool, cut and serve. Refrigerate any unlikely leftovers.

Cheese & Veggie Chews

½ c grated cheese
3 T olive or vegetable oil
3 tsp applesauce
½ c cooked veggies (dog's favorite)
1 c flour
Milk (skim or 2% are okay)

Mix cheese, oil, applesauce, and veggies together. Stir in flour thoroughly. Add just enough milk to form dough into a ball. Cover and refrigerate one hour. Roll on floured surface and cut into cookie cutter shapes. Bake at 375°F for 15 minutes. Cool and store extras in refrigerator or freezer.

Cheesy Twists

1 extra-large egg, beaten
¾ c beef or chicken broth (canned AOK)
3/4 c grated parmesan cheese, divided
2 c flour (white or whole wheat or combo)
¼ c cornmeal

Mix egg with broth; stir in ¼ cup of cheese. Add flour and cornmeal. Mix thoroughly and roll into 1" balls, then into sticks. On surface sprinkled with remaining cheese, coat each with Parmesan. Twist sticks a few times and place on ungreased baking sheet. Bake at 325°F for 25-30 minutes. Cool and store in refrigerator or freezer.

Cheesy Cookies

2 c flour
1¼ c shredded cheddar cheese
1 T freshly chopped parsley
½ c vegetable oil

Combine all ingredients. Add 5-6 tablespoons of water until the mixture forms a ball. On a floured surface, roll to ½" thickness and cut into cookie cutter shapes. Place on ungreased baking sheets. Bake at 400°F for 10 min. Store in refrigerator or freezer.

Chicken Liver Squares

1 lb. chicken livers, boiled
½ c beef broth (canned AOK)
1 extra-large egg, beaten
1 c flour
1 c corn meal
1 T freshly chopped parsley

Place livers and broth in blender; process till smooth. Add egg and blend 1 minute. Pour into medium bowl and mix in flour, corn meal and parsley. Pour mixture into greased pan with sides. Bake at 400°F for 15 minutes. While still warm, cut into small, bite-sized squares. Store in freezer in daily portion quantities in small plastic bags.

Note: These are favorites, both frozen and thawed.

Chewy Chicken Licken's

2 c flour (white or whole wheat combo)
1 c cornmeal
1 extra-large egg, beaten
2 T vegetable oil
½ c chicken broth (or liquid from boiling livers)
2 T chopped fresh parsley
1 c cooked chicken livers, chopped

Combine flour and cornmeal in small bowl. In a medium bowl, mix egg with oil, broth, parsley and livers. Add flour combo to the liquid mixture a little at a time, stirring well after each addition. On a floured surface, roll to ½" thick and cut into squares. Place on greased baking sheet. Bake at 350°F for 15 minutes. Store in refrigerator or freezer.

Baked Bow Wow Meatballs

½ lb ground beef
¼ c grated cheese
1 carrot, grated
½ c soft bread crumbs
1 extra-large egg, beaten
1 T tomato paste

Mix all ingredients together thoroughly. Roll into meatballs (tiny or up to 2"). Place on greased baking sheet. Bake at 350°F for 15-20 minutes, depending on size of meatballs. They should be brown and firm. Cool and store in the refrigerator or freezer.

Bacon Bites

¼ c bacon fat, softened
1 extra-large egg
1 T freshly chopped parsley
4 slices crisply cooked bacon, crumbled
½ c chilled beef broth or cold water
½ c milk
3 c flour (white or whole wheat)

Cream bacon fat; stir in egg, then parsley, bacon, broth, and milk. Mix in flour thoroughly. On floured surface, roll dough to ¼ to ½" thickness and cut in cookie cutter shapes or bite-sized squares. Place on lightly greased baking sheet. Bake at 325°F for 30-35 minutes. Cool and store in refrigerator or freezer.

Sloppy Bones

2 c dried dog food (crunchies)
1 can wet dog food
3 coarsely broken dog biscuits
3 crumbled crisply cooked bacon strips

Stir canned food into the dry crunchies. Stir in biscuits and bacon.

Note: Makes 2-3 servings for large dogs, like the Miles-Mannered Man. It makes many more for small dogs. Store in a sealed container in the refrigerator.

Upgraded Cheap Cookies

I've told you how I <u>love</u> what we call "Cheap Cookies." Okay, they're called "ice cubes" in human lingo. They are GREAT in the summer, especially. However, for variety, try this super upgrade.

2 cans chicken or beef broth
Small pieces of cooked chicken or beef

Place a bit (or 2) of chicken or beef in each ice cube tray. Pour broth over and freeze. AWESOME!!!

Note: Except for really large dogs, only fill each ice cube tray ¼ to ½ full. Also... you can use just one can of broth with one can of water, if you prefer an "enlightened" cookie. (Ha-ha-ha... even we dogs can do plays on words!)

Veggie Pops

Your dog's favorite fruits and vegetables, cooked or raw.

Cut up the fruits and veggies in small pieces and put in ice cube trays. Pour water over the fruits and veggies. (Only fill to ¼ or ½ full if your doggie is small.) Once frozen, store in closed plastic bags in the freezer.

Note: Some favorite Miles-Mannered Man combinations:
- Carrots and bananas
- Green string beans and tomatoes
- Apples and peanuts

Fruity Pops

2 soft bananas, mashed
½ c plain yogurt
1 qt dog's favorite fruit juice (such as apple)

Mix bananas and yogurt together; stir in fruit juice. Spoon into ice cube trays. Once frozen, store in closed plastic bags in the freezer.

Note: Among the Miles-Mannered Man's favorite juices are pear and apricot. Uh… and my humans like them, too.

Peanut Butter Pops
1½ c peanut butter, creamy or chunky
32-oz container of plain or vanilla yogurt

Microwave the peanut butter briefly to melt it. Mix in the yogurt. Pour into cupcake papers and freeze on baking sheets. (For small dogs, use the mini candy papers.) Once frozen, store in closed plastic bags in the freezer.

Peanut Butter Balls
Peanut butter (creamy or chunky)
Quick oats

Take a spoonful of peanut butter and coat it in oats. Make as many as you'd like and then freeze on wax paper lined baking sheets. Once frozen, store in closed plastic bags in the freezer.

Note: If your dog is very small, you can cut them into little pieces. Oh, and it is okay to share with your humans, too.

Peanut Butter Munchies

2 c quick oats
2 c hot water
1 c peanut butter (chunky is best)
¼ c banana chips
4 c flour (white or whole wheat or combo)

Stir oats into hot water. Cream into peanut butter. Stir in banana chips and flour. (Add more flour if the dough is too sticky to handle.) Knead together. On floured surface roll to ¼" thick and cut into cookie cutter shapes. Place 1" apart on greased baking sheet. Bake at 350°F for 30-40 minutes. Let them cool thoroughly.

Peanut Butter Patties

1/3 c peanut butter (creamy or chunky)
2 extra-large eggs, beaten
2 tsp vanilla
¼ c vegetable oil
¼ c applesauce
1½ c water
3 c flour (white or whole wheat combo)
1 c cornmeal
¾ c quick oats

Cream peanut butter and eggs; stir in vanilla. Mix in oil and applesauce, then water. In a large bowl, mix together the flour, cornmeal and oats. Stir in the wet ingredients until mixed thoroughly. Roll dough in a ball. On floured surface, roll to ½" thickness. Cut into cookie cutter shapes and place on ungreased baking sheet. Bake at 400°F for 15 minutes. Then, simply turn oven off and leave patties in closed oven for 1 hour to crisp.

Note: Store cookies at room temperatures, but not in a sealed container, unless you want them to be softer.

Bowzer Brownies

½ c Crisco shortening
3 T honey
4 extra-large eggs
1 tsp vanilla
1 c flour
¼ c carob powder (NOT chocolate)
½ tsp baking powder

Frosting:
8 oz fat free cream cheese, softened
2-3 tsp honey

Cream shortening and honey; stir in eggs and vanilla; beat well. Mix in dry ingredients, stirring well. Press into large greased brownie pan. Bake 25 minutes at 350°F. Cool. Blend frosting ingredients together and spread over cooled brownies. Cut in squares, from 1½" to 3", depending on your dog's size.

Canine Banana Ice Cream

1 large container of fat-free plain or vanilla yogurt (or Greek)
2 large soft bananas, mashed
¾ c water

Mix ingredients well. Pour into cupcake papers or small paper cups and freeze on baking sheets. (For small dogs, use mini candy papers.) Once frozen, store in closed plastic bags in the freezer.

Extra Treat #4

DOG JOKES & QUOTES WITH THE MILES PAW OF APPROVAL 🐾

These are both sage thoughts and silliness that I've collected over the years. I hope you enjoy them. They make me smile and my humans have laughed right along with me. I let them read dog stories and jokes and such to me. It's very relaxing. Maybe that's the reading material; maybe it's because they pat me while they read to me. I just know I like it. Hope you do, too.

When a man's best friend is his dog, that dog has a problem.
-- Edward Abbey, American Author (1927 – 1989)

The difference between cats and dogs is dogs come when they are called; cats take a message and get back to you.
-- Anonymous

Cat's motto: *No matter what you've done wrong, always try to make it look like the dog did it.*
-- Unknown

Just give me a comfortable couch, a dog, a good book, and a woman. Then if you can get the dog to go somewhere and read the book, I might have a little fun!
-- Groucho Marx, American Comedian (1895-1977)

The Evolution of Dog Rules

1. The dog is not allowed in the house.
2. Okay, the dog is allowed in the house, but only in certain rooms.
3. The dog is allowed in all rooms, but has to stay off the furniture.
4. The dog can get on the old furniture only.
5. Fine, the dog is allowed on all the furniture, but is not allowed to sleep with the humans on the bed.
6. Okay, the dog is allowed on the bed, but only by invitation.
7. The dog can sleep on the bed whenever he wants, but not under the covers.
8. The dog can sleep under the covers by invitation only.
9. The dog can sleep under the covers every night.
10. Humans must ask permission to sleep under the covers with the dog.

Some days you're the dog; some days you're the hydrant.
-- Unknown

I went to a movie theater the other day and saw an old man and his dog in the front row.

It was a sad/funny kind of film. During the sad parts, the dog cried his eyes out, and during the funny parts, the dog laughed his head off. This happened all the way through the movie.

When it ended, I walked up to the man and said, "That's the most amazing thing I've ever seen. Your dog really seemed to enjoy the film."

The man turned to me and said, "Yeah, it is. He hated the book."

Jesus Is Watching

A burglar broke into a house one night. Sneaking around, he suddenly heard, "Jesus is watching you!"

The burglar was shocked, ducked down, and remained silent for a while, but nothing happened. After a minute or so of silence, he got up again.

Then, a little louder, he heard a warning tone, "Jesus is still watching you!"

"Good heavens!" he thought. "What's going on here?"

Silently he stepped forward again, and really loud this time he heard, "Jesus is *really* watching you!"

The burglar was almost ready to have a heart attack. He switched on his flashlight, looked around and saw a parrot.

Burglar: "A parrot?"

Parrot: "Yes, that's me!"

Burglar: "You can talk pretty well!"

Parrot: "Yes, I'm already 50 years of age."

Burglar: "Phew! I really thought something weird was going on here! What's your name?"

Parrot: "Henry."

Burglar: "Henry? That's a weird name for a parrot."

Parrot: "Not as weird as 'Jesus' for a Rottweiler."

*My sunshine doesn't come from the skies;
it comes from the love in my dog's eyes.*
            -- Unknown

You know why dogs have no money? No pockets. 'Cause they see change on the street all the time and it's driving them crazy. When you're walking them, he is always looking up at you. "There's a quarter..."
            -- Jerry Seinfeld, American Comedian (1954 -)

Once you let a dog into your heart, it will live there forever.

Dog's Duty

A nursery school teacher was delivering a station wagon full of kids home one day when a fire truck zoomed past. Sitting in the front passenger seat of the fire truck was a Dalmation dog. The children started discussing the dog's duties.

"They use him to keep crowds back," said one youngster.

"No," said another. "He's just for good luck."

A third child firmly closed the argument with, "They use the dogs to find the fire hydrant."

*There is no psychiatrist in the world
like a puppy licking your face.*
            -- Sir Bernard Williams,
            English Philosopher (1929-2003)

The nose of the Bulldog has been slanted backwards so that he can breathe without letting go.
         -- Winston Churchill, English Statesman /
              Prime Minister (1874-1965)

He is your friend, your partner, your defender, your dog.
You are his life, his love, his leader.
He will be yours, faithful and true,
to the last beat of his heart.
You owe it to him to be worthy of such devotion.
                  -- Unknown

If your dog doesn't like someone
you probably shouldn't either.
                  --Unknown

Acquiring a dog may be the only opportunity a human ever has to choose a relative.
               -- Mordecai Siegal,
          American Pet Writer (1935-2010)

I spilled spot remover on my dog. He's gone now.
       -- Steven Wright, American Comedian (1955 -)

*You always sympathize with the underdog,
except when the other dog is yours.*
                                              -- Anonymous

If you can start every day without caffeine or pills...
If you can be cheerful, ignoring aches and pains...
If you can resist complaining and boring people with your troubles...
If you can eat the same food every day and be grateful for it...
If you can understand when loved ones are too busy to give you enough time...
If you can overlook it when people take frustrations out on you, when something has gone wrong through no fault of yours...
If you can take criticism and blame, without resentment...
If you can face the world without lies and deceit...
If you can conquer stress and tension without medical help...
If you can always relax without liquor and sleep without the aid of drugs...
Then....
You're probably a dog.

*Did you hear about the dyslexic agnostic insomniac who
stays up all night wondering if there really is a Dog?*

On judgment day, if God should say,
"Did you clean your house today?"
I will say, "I did not.
I played with my dogs, and I forgot."

Dogs feel very strongly that they should always go with you in the car, in case the need should arise for them to bark violently at nothing right in your ear.
     -- David Barry, Pulitzer Prize-Winning American Humorist & Author (1947 -)

Things to do today:
1. FEED THE GOOD DOG
2. PET THE GOOD DOG
3. GIVE the GOOD DOG A TREAT
4. Take pens & pencils away from the dog

Canine Creation Theory
On the first day God created the dog.
On the second day, God created man to serve the dog.
On the third day, God created all the animals of the earth to serve as potential food for the dog.
On the fourth day, God created honest toil so that man could labor for the good of the dog.
On the fifth day, God created the tennis ball so that the dog might or might not retrieve it.
On the sixth day, God created veterinary science to keep the dog healthy & the man broke.
On the seventh day, God tried to rest, but he had to walk the dog.

A Man and His Dog

A man and his dog were walking along a road. The man was enjoying the scenery, when it suddenly occurred to him that he was dead. He remembered dying and that the dog had been dead for years. After a while they came to a high, white stonewall. It looked like fine marble. At the top of a long hill was a tall arch that glowed in the sunlight. When he was standing before it he saw a magnificent gate in the arch that looked like mother of pearl, and the street that led to the gate looked like pure gold. He and the dog walked toward the gate, and as he got closer he saw a man at a desk to one side. When he was close enough he called out, "Excuse me, where are we?"

"This is Heaven, sir," the man answered. "Wow! Would you happen to have some water?" the man asked.

"Of course, sir. Come right in. I'll have some ice water brought right up." The man gestured, and the gate began to open."

Can my dog come in too?" the traveler asked. "I'm sorry, sir, but we don't accept pets," came the reply.

The man thought for a moment, then turned away; they continued down the road. After another long walk, and at the top of a long hill, he came to a dirt road leading through a farm gate that looked as if it had never been closed. There was no fence. As he approached the gate he saw a man inside, leaning against a tree and reading a book.

"Excuse me" he called to the reader, "Do you have any water?"

"Yeah, sure, there's a pump over there." The man pointed and said, "Come on in."

"How about my friend here?" the traveler gestured to the dog.

"There should be a bowl by the pump."

They went through the gate and, sure enough, there was an old-fashioned hand pump with a bowl beside it. The traveler filled the bowl and took a long drink himself. Then he gave some to the dog. When they were full, he and the dog walked back toward the man, who was standing by then, waiting for them. "What do you call this place?" the traveler asked.

"This is Heaven," was the answer.

"Well, that's confusing," the traveler said. "The man down the road said **that** was Heaven."

"Oh, you mean the place with the gold street and pearly gates? Nope. That's Hell."

"Doesn't it make you mad for them to use your name like that?"

"No. I can see how you might think so, but we're just happy that they screen out the folks who'll leave their dogs behind."

Don't accept your dog's admiration as conclusive evidence that you are wonderful.
-- Ann Landers (Esther Friedman Lederer)
American Advice Columnist (1918 – 2002)

*My husband and I are either going to
buy a dog or have a child.
We can't decide whether to ruin our carpets or ruin our lives.*
-- Rita Rudner, American Comedian (1956 -)

*I have found that when you are deeply troubled there are
things you get from the silent devoted companionship of a dog
that you can get from no other source.*
--Doris Day, American Singer & Actress,
Animal Rights Advocate (1924 -)

*If you have men who will exclude any of God's creatures
from the shelter of compassion and pity,
you will have men who will deal likewise
with their fellow men.*
-- St. Francis of Assisi, Italian,
Founder of Franciscan Order (1182 – 1226)

*No man can be condemned for owning a dog.
As long as he has a dog, he has a friend;
and the poorer he gets, the better friends he has.*
-- Will Rogers, American Humorist (1879-1935)

How many dogs does it take to put in a light bulb?

Golden Retriever: The sun is shining, the day is young, we've got our whole lives ahead of us, and you're inside worrying about a stupid burned-out light bulb?

Border Collie: One. And I'll replace any wiring not up to code.

Dachshund: I can't reach the stupid lamp!

Newfoundland: Man, I'm trying, but I can't hold the bulb... it's that 'no thumbs' thing again.

Toy Poodle: I'll just blow in the Border collie's ear; he'll do it. When he finishes rewiring the house, my nails will be dry.

Rottweiler: Go ahead! Make me!

Shih tzu: Puh-leeze, dah-ling. Let the servants do it.

Labrador Retriever: Oh, me, **me**!!! *Choose me*. Let ME change the light bulb! Please, please, please! Can I? Can I? Huh? Huh? Can I?

Cocker Spaniel: Why? I can still pee on the carpet in the dark.

Doberman Pinscher: While it's dark, I'll sleep on the couch.

Mastiff: Mastiffs are NOT afraid of the dark.

Hound Dog: ZZZZZZZZZZZZZZZZZZZZ

Chihuahua: Yo quiero Taco Bulb.

Irish Wolfhound: Not me. I've got a hangover.

Pointer: I see it, there it is, right there. Look at that.

Greyhound: It isn't moving. Who cares?

Old English Sheep Dog: Light bulb? Light bulb? That thing I just ate was a light bulb?

Pomeranian: Dogs do not change light bulbs. People change light bulbs. I am not one of them, so the question is: how long will it be before I can expect light.

A lawyer is just like an attack dog, only without a conscience.
  -- Tom Clancy, American Author (1947-   )

Dog Property Laws

- If I like it, it's mine.
- If it's in my mouth, it's mine.
- If I can take it from you, it's mine.
- If I had it a little while ago, it's mine.
- If it's mine, it must never appear to be yours in any way.
- If I'm chewing something up, all the pieces are mine.
- If it just looks like mine, it's mine.
- If I saw it first, it's mine.
- If you are playing with something and you put it down, it automatically becomes mine.
- If it's broken, it's yours.

The greatness of a nation and its moral progress can be judged by the way its animals are treated.
  -- Gandhi, Indian Political & Spiritual Leader (1869-1948)

When a dog bites a man that is not news, but when a man bites a dog that is news.
  -- Charles Anderson Dana, American Journalist (1819-1897)

I bought a dog the other day... I named him Stay. It's fun to call him... "Come here, Stay! Come here, Stay!" He went insane. Now he just ignores me and keeps typing.
  -- Steven Wright, American Comedian (1955-   )

Beware of Dog!

Upon entering the little country store, the stranger noticed a sign saying, "DANGER! BEWARE OF DOG!" posted on the glass door. Inside he saw a harmless old hound dog asleep on the floor beside the cash register.

He asked the store manager, "Is THAT the dog folks are supposed to beware of?"

"Yep, that's him," he replied.

The stranger couldn't help but be amused. "That certainly doesn't look like a dangerous dog to me. Why in the world would you post that sign?"

"Because," the owner replied, "before I posted that sign, people kept tripping over him."

It is not the size of the dog in the fight; it's the size of the fight in the dog.
-- Dwight Eisenhower, 34th U.S. President 1953-1961
(1890-1969)
(Quote also credited to Mark Twain)

The more people I meet the more I like my dog.
-- Unknown

No one appreciates the very special genius of your conversation as the dog does.
-- Christopher Morley,
American Journalist (1890-1957)

Of all the things I miss from veterinary practice, puppy breath is one of the fondest memories!
-- Dr. Tom Cat (Thomas E. Catanzaro),
American Veterinary Consultant (1944-)

I've seen a look in dogs' eyes, a quickly vanishing look of amazed contempt, and I am convinced that basically dogs think humans are nuts.
-- John Steinbeck, Nobel and Pulitzer Prize-Winning American Author (1902-1968)

Anybody who doesn't know what soap tastes like never washed a dog.
-- Franklin P. Jones,
American Businessman (1887-1929)

Two duck hunters were arguing over who had the better dog. So they decide to take them out together in the boat to settle it, with $50 going to the winner.

They call a couple birds in and the first hunter shoots them both, his dog sitting rock solid marking them. The first hunter sends his dog, who proceeds to make two picture perfect retrieves from 100 yards plus with no handling instructions.

The second hunter after watching this performance doesn't look concerned at all. He starts calling and a couple of birds come into range, and he knocks them down clean. He looks at the first hunter and says, "Watch this." He sends his dog, who steps out of the boat and walks across the water and brings both birds back.

The second hunter turns to the first hunter and says, "Give me my $50."

The first hunter looks him in the eye and says, "Are you kidding me? That dog can't even swim!"

*The dog has seldom been successful
in pulling man up to its level of sagacity,
but man has frequently dragged the dog down to his.*
-- James Thurber,
American Humorist (1894-1961)

Dogs' lives are too short. Their only fault, really.
-- Agnes Sligh Turnbull,
American Author (1888-1992)

*A dog is the only thing on this earth
that loves you more than he loves himself.*
-- Josh Billings (Henry Wheeler Shaw),
American Humorist (1818-1885)

*I consciously choose the dog's path through life.
I shall be poor; I shall be a painter.*
-- Vincent van Gogh,
Dutch Artist (1853-1890)

*Dogs. They are better than human beings,
because they know but do not tell.*
-- Emily Dickinson,
American Poet **(1830-1886)**

*Politics are not my concern…
they impressed me as a dog's life without a dog's decencies.*
-- Rudyard Kipling,
British Author (1865-1936)

The Top 20 Reasons Dogs Don't Use Computers

20. Can't stick their heads out of Windows '95.

19. Fetch command not available on all platforms.

18. Hard to read monitor with your head cocked to one side.

17. Too difficult to "mark" every web site they visit.

16. Can't help attacking the screen when they hear, "You've Got Mail."

15. Fire hydrant icon is simply frustrating.

14. Involuntary tail wagging is dead giveaway they're browsing www.pethouse.com instead of working.

13. Keep bruising noses trying to catch that MPEG frisbee.

12. Not at all fooled by Chuck Wagon Screen Saver.

11. Still trying to come up with an "emotion icon" that signifies tail-wagging.

10. Waiting for the bone to replace the mouse.

9. Three words: Carpal Paw Syndrome

8. Because dogs ain't GEEKS! Now, cats, on the other hand...

7. Barking in next cube keeps activating YOUR voice recognition software.

6. Spell check function still does not recognize dog languages.

5. SIT and STAY were hard enough; SAVE and SEND are too weird.

4. Saliva-coated mouse slips out of mouth.

3. Annoyed by lack of canine news groups and dogs' blogs.

2. Butt-sniffing is more direct and less deceiving than online chat rooms.

and the Number 1 Reason Dogs Don't Use Computers...
1. **Cr{gA Ns'[T,bTY PyAq4tEc Wgro IgTm HeIjy P;AzWqS.** *
(* 1. Can't Type With Paws!)

In a town filled with crime, a young married couple was worried after 3 of their neighbors' homes had been burglarized. They decided they should get a guard dog. The wife went to the local pet store and asked the assistant, "Do you have any guard dogs?" The sales assistant replied, "Sorry Madam; we're all sold out. All we have left is a Scottie Dog, but he does know Karate."

The wife didn't believe him, so the clerk says to the dog, "Karate the chair." The little dog then goes up to the chair and whack, he brakes it into tiny pieces. Then he said to the dog, "Karate that table." The dog went to the table and crunch, he breaks it in half.

So, the wife bought the dog and took it home to her husband, who was expecting a big, traditional guard dog. He was, of course, very disappointed and skeptical about this little dog's ability as a guard dog.

When she informed him that the dog knew Karate, he laughed and said, "Karate my a$$!"

Yeah… the husband is still recovering.

I would rather see the portrait of a dog that I know, than all the allegorical paintings they can show me in the world.
-- Samuel Johnson,
English Poet & Essayist (1709-1784)

If you eliminate smoking and gambling, you will be amazed to find that almost all an Englishman's pleasures can be, and mostly are, shared by his dog.
-- George Bernard Shaw, Nobel Prize-Winning Irish Playwright (1856-1950)

Help Wanted

A local business was looking for office help. He put a sign in the window, stating the following:

> **HELP WANTED**
> - **Must be able to type**
> - **Must be good with a computer**
> - **Must be bilingual.**
>
> **We are an Equal Opportunity Employer.**

A short time afterwards, a dog trotted up to the window, saw the sign and went inside. He looked at the receptionist and wagged his tail, then walked over to the sign, looked at it and whined. Getting the idea, the receptionist got the office manager. He looked at the dog with surprise, but the dog looked determined, so he lead him into the office. Inside, the dog jumped up on the chair and stared at the manager.

The manager said, "I can't hire you. The sign says you have to be able to type." The dog jumped down, went to the typewriter and proceeded to type out a perfect letter. He took out the page and trotted over to give it to the manager, and then he jumped back on the chair.

The manager was stunned, but then said to the dog, "The sign says you have to be good with a computer." The dog jumped down went to the computer and proceeded to demonstrate his expertise with various programs and produced a sample spreadsheet and database and presented them to the manager.

By this time the manager was totally dumb-founded! He looked at the dog and said, "I realize that you are a very intelligent dog and have some fascinating abilities. But, I STILL can't give you the job." The dog jumped down and went to a copy of the sign and put his paw on the sentence about being an Equal Opportunity Employer.

The manager said, "Yes, but it *also* says that you must be bilingual." The dog looked at him straight in the face and said, "Meow."

Time spent with a dog is never wasted.

The American Kennel Club is reportedly reviewing the following proposed breeds:
- Collie + Lhasa Apso = Collapso, a dog that folds up for easy carrying
- Spitz + Chow Chow = Spitz-Chow, a dog that throws up a lot
- Pointer + Setter = Poinsetter, a traditional Christmas pet
- Great Pyrenees + Dachshund = Pyradachs, a puzzling breed
- Pekingnese + Lhasa Apso = Peekasso, an abstract dog
- Irish Water Spaniel + English Springer Spaniel = Irish Springer, a dog fresh and clean as a whistle
- Labrador Retriever + Curly Coated Retriever = Lab Coat Retriever, the choice of research scientists
- Newfoundland + Basset Hound = Newfound Asset Hound, a dog for financial advisors
- Terrier + Bulldog = Terribull, a dog that makes awful mistakes
- Bloodhound + Labrador = Blabador, a dog that barks incessantly
- Malamute + Pointer = Moot Point, owned by....oh, well, it doesn't matter anyway
- Kerry Blue Terrier + Skye Terrier = Blue Skye, a dog for visionaries
- Collie + Malamute = Commute, a dog that travels to work
- Deerhound + Terrier = Derriere, a dog that's true to the end

Histories are more full of examples
of the fidelity of dogs than of friends.
-- Alexander Pope,
English Poet (1688-1744)

I wonder if other dogs think poodles
are members of a weird religious cult.
-- Rita Rudner,
American Comedian (1956-)

Dogs are our link to paradise.
They don't know evil or jealousy or discontent.
To sit with a dog on a hillside on a glorious afternoon
is to be back in Eden,
where doing nothing was not boring--it was peace.
-- Milan Kundera,
Czechoslovakian Author (1929-)

Money will buy a pretty good dog,
but it won't buy the wag of his tail.
-- Josh Billings (Henry Wheeler Shaw),
American Humorist (1818-1885)

In order to really enjoy a dog,
one doesn't merely try to train him to be semi-human.
The point of it is to open oneself
to the possibility of becoming partly a dog.
-- Edward Hoagland,
American Author (1932-)

A Dog's Personal Dictionary & Guide

Leash: A strap that attaches to your collar, enabling you to lead your humans where you want them to go. Make sure that you are waiting patiently with leash in mouth when your humans come home from work. This immediately makes them feel guilty and lengthens the walk by a good 10 minutes.

Dog Bed: Any soft, clean surface, such as a white bedspread, newly upholstered couch, the dry cleaning that was just picked up, or your human's feet.

Drool: What you do when your owners have food and you don't. To do this properly, sit as close as you can to them, look sad, and let the drool fall to the floor... or, better yet, on their laps.

Sniff: A social custom that is always proper to use when you greet other dogs or special people that interest you.

Garbage Can: A container that humans put out weekly to test your ingenuity. Stand on your hind legs and push the lid off with your nose. If you do it right, you are rewarded with food wrappers to shred, beef bones to consume, moldy crusts of bread and sometimes even an old Nike sneaker to gnaw.

Bicycles: Two-wheeled exercise machines to control dogs' body fat. For maximum aerobic benefit, you must hide behind a bush and dash out, bark loudly and run alongside a bicycle for a few yards. The rider swerves and falls into the bushes, and you prance away. Exercise isn't supposed to be fun, but this is GREAT.

Thunder: A signal the world is coming to an end. Humans remain amazingly calm during thunderstorms, so it is necessary to warn them of the danger by trembling, whining, panting, rolling your eyes wildly and following VERY closely at their heels.

Wastebasket: A dog toy box filled with paper, envelopes and old candy wrappers. When you get bored, turn over the basket and strew the papers all over the house. This is particularly fun to do when there are guests for dinner and you prance around with the contents of that very special bathroom wastepaper basket!

Sofas: Sofas are to dogs what napkins are to people. After eating it is polite to run up and down the front of the sofa to wipe your whiskers clean. If there are people sitting on the couch just include them as a handy wipe.

Bath: A process owners use to clean you, drench the floor, walls and themselves. You can help by shaking vigorously and frequently. Barking and jumping around is also helpful.

Rub: Every good dog's response to the command "sit," especially if your owner is dressed for an evening out. This is incredibly effective before black-tie events.

Love: A feeling of intense affection, given freely and without restriction, shared by you and your humans. Show your love by wagging your tail, kissing your humans, and running to them gleefully each and every time they return home to you.

CREDITS & REFERENCES

Research for quotes, pets, history, and heroes for Miles' bonus "extras" chapters was very carefully done. We apologize if any details are inconsistent with information you may have heard or read elsewhere. When varying sources had different accountings of stories, all possible attempts were made to verify.

Photograph credits and my most paws-itive gratitude go to Cathy Martin, Nina Martin, and Ryan Jarnutowski. (Plus a couple of other friends.)

Presidential Pets
Dwight D. Eisenhower Library Center
en.wikipedia.org
Franklin D. Roosevelt Presidential Library and Museum
Illinois State Historical Library
John F. Kennedy Library
L.B.J. Library
Library of Congress
"Lincoln's Dog Fido" story
MSNBC
National Geographic
Presidential Pets Museum
Ronald Reagan Foundation & Library
Smithsonian Magazine
Washington Post
White House Library
www.factmonster.com
www.infoplease.com

www.pethall.com
www.pets-in-the-news.com
www.presidentialmuseums.com
www.presidentsusa.net
www.simplyfamily.com
www.whitehouse.gov
www.whitehousekids.gov

Famous & Heroic Dogs
American Kennel Club — Newfoundland
Associated Press
CNN
Heinz Pet Products
Humane Society of the United States
NCA
Newfoundland Dog Club of America
Newfoundland Dog Club of Canada
Newfoundland Dog Club of Ohio
New York Times
Westminster Kennel Club
www.animalgazette.com
www.capricciofarmnewfs.com
www.canismajor.com
www.dogsinthenews.com
www.hdserv.com
www.myhero.com
www.newfoundland-dogs.com
www.northernmaritimeresearch.com
www.pets-in-the-news.com
www.rewarddog.com
www.skippydog.com
Various Newfoundland dog-oriented blogs

Recipes, Jokes & Quotes
www.animalgazette.com
www.dakotanewfoundlands.com
www.dogs-care.com

Special thanks to all of my humans' friends and family who provided special notes, poems, stories, photos, recipes, quotes and jokes to be included in the **Miles-Mannered Man**.

For more information, articles, free recipes, and additional titles, join the conversation at
www.GoodLiving123.com.

Visit the Quiet Thunder Publishing website:
www.QTPublishing.com